"No fears as long as we work together"

Follow Up Joint Inspection of Scottish Borders Council and NHS Borders

Verifying implementation of their action plan for services for people with learning disabilities

The action plan is the response to the Social Work Services Inspectorate and Mental Welfare Commission Reports (May 2004) into the abuse of a number of vulnerable adults with learning disabilities

Social Work Inspection Agency
Edinburgh 2005

362.3

T28025

CONTENTS

Accessible summary
written by Brian Rosie, Mary Anderson and Ursula Corker (with the support of People First)

Background

In May 2004, the Social Work Services Inspectorate (SWSI) and the Mental Welfare Commission for Scotland published reports about the abuse of a number of vulnerable adults with learning disabilities who live in the Borders. These reports said there were serious failings in Scottish Borders Council and NHS Borders services for people with learning disabilities. The reports made 33 recommendations for Scottish Borders Council, NHS Borders and their partners (some recommendations apply to all local authorities and NHS Boards in Scotland). On 6 May 2004, the Minister for Education and Young People said there would be a follow up joint inspection to check if Scottish Borders Council, NHS Borders and their partners were carrying out their action plan. Scottish Borders Council, NHS Borders and their partners wrote an action plan, saying how they would make the 33 recommendations happen. This is our report of the follow up inspection.

This was a joint inspection, led by the Social Work Inspection Agency and the Mental Welfare Commission.

Two people with learning disabilities and a family carer were inspectors on the inspection team. We had representatives on the inspection team from:

People First (Scotland)
Carers Scotland
The Care Commission
NHS Quality Improvement Scotland,
HM Inspectorate of Education
HM Inspectorate of Constabulary
Audit Scotland

Brian and Mary say

It was good that people with learning disabilities were asked to be inspectors. We could relate to the situations that people with learning disabilities find themselves in if they use services. We spoke to health and social work staff and to workers from voluntary organisations.

Being able to speak to people face to face was important. We were able to listen to what was good for people and what was not so good for them. We could see that things are getting better for people and that they were being listened to.

We hope this inspection will help to make things better for people with learning disabilities.

Ursula says

As a carer, being involved in the inspection was interesting and rewarding. It was hard work.

It allowed carers who were interviewed the opportunity to speak with someone who understands what being a carer means, the pressures, stresses and joys.

NHS Borders and Scottish Borders Council responded to the recommendations in the Social Work Services Inspectorate (SWSI) and Mental Welfare Commission reports in 2004.

They produced a very full action plan. The inspection team looked at how well this plan was working. The inspection team visited the Borders in the week 9 May to 13 May 2005.

We think the changes are working. We think services in the Borders have done very well with the actions they have taken. We found some things they still need to do.

A word about tense

This follow up inspection report mainly uses the past tense, for example there **was** a huge effort. We state the position at the time of the follow up inspection. This does not mean the stated position is no longer the case. So when we say there **was** a huge effort (at the time of the inspection) we do not mean there is **no longer** a huge effort. If something was happening but is not happening now, we say so.

Summary of main points of the Borders Follow Up Inspection Report

There has been a huge effort by all agencies to act on the recommendations from the Social Work Services Inspectorate and Mental Welfare Commission reports. We were impressed with how much work everyone put in. We thank them for the excellent help we got.

In the abuse of the vulnerable adults who live in the Borders case, there were key points when Scottish Borders Council and NHS Borders could have acted decisively to protect the victims and they did not.

We have produced a chart that shows what would happen if these key events occurred now. There is now a much greater chance of agencies:
- finding out about the abuse of adults with learning disabilities; and
- stopping the abuse once they find out about it.

It is also more likely agencies will prevent adults with learning disabilities being abused.

We say what Scottish Borders Council, NHS Borders and their partners still need to do to make sure adults with learning disabilities are even safer.

We asked Borders Independent Advocacy Service (BIAS) and the Scottish Consortium for Learning Disability (SCLD) to do a survey of people with learning disabilities and family carers in the Borders. Main findings:

- *Support and choice:* Good relationships with staff. Choice could be increased.

- *Having a say:* Some people have gained a great deal from participation. The benefits of this should go to more people. People could benefit from personal life plans. They should have copies of them. People should get more information about advocacy and how to get in touch with advocacy organisations.

- *Social workers:* Most people had a good relationship with their social worker. They thought their social workers would help keep them safe. Three people said they did not have a social worker.

- *Feeling safe:* All adults surveyed said they knew someone to contact if they were frightened. People are safer if they have contacts in the wider community and if people know and care about them.

- **_Health:_** People knew about healthy lifestyles. There are very good reports of doctors and hospitals.

- **_Quality of life:_** Most people said they had the life they wanted. Some had few opportunities and poor networks.

We found good leadership and management in Scottish Borders Council, the social work department and NHS Borders.

Most carers we spoke to felt things were getting better. Carers knew the social worker. They were happy with the service they got from the social worker. The Scottish Executive sees carers as "partners in care". Carers should be inspectors.

The Princess Royal Trust for Carers, NHS Borders and Scottish Borders Council have written a good carer's assessment form. Carers saw the benefits of a carer's assessment.

People with learning disabilities are more involved in the planning and delivery of their services.

All agencies knew about *The same as you?* policies.

Most staff we spoke to (all agencies) see people with learning disabilities as equal citizens and treat them with respect.

Multi-agency training on protecting vulnerable adults has been very good. Lots of staff have been trained. We found nearly all staff knew about protecting vulnerable adults

Scottish Borders Council and NHS Borders have done a lot of work to improve policies and procedures to help keep adults with learning disabilities safe.

The social work department and NHS Borders have tried hard to make their record keeping better. Social workers now keep much better records since the social work department checked all learning disability records in April 2004.

Joint working among agencies is much better. There is sharing of information. There is a system to sort out disagreements.

Social workers know about codes of practice. Social work records showed practice is getting better. Social workers called case meetings. They wrote down things to be done to protect vulnerable adults with learning disabilities.

Mental health officers are better trained and supervised. Their practice and knowledge is better.

NHS learning disability services are better led. They have good links with primary care services, GPs and hospitals.

Some staff in GP practices still treat people with learning disabilities differently to everyone else. Record keeping and communication were better. There was better transfer of information between GP practices.

We found better practice and communication at Borders General Hospital. The liaison nurse helped to make things better for people with learning disabilities and their families.

The voluntary and private sectors are involved in Scottish Borders Council and NHS Borders plans to protect vulnerable adults with learning disabilities.

We found some difficulties with services for children and young people with learning disabilities who are at the change-over stage between early years and school years and between children services and adult services. Service planning and review should involve all agencies. Services should be more user friendly to meet children and young people's education, support and leisure needs.

Higher level management should give even more attention to what is going on. Social work senior managers need to look at more protection of vulnerable adults with learning disabilities case files and staff supervision records.

Team leaders had not regularly looked at and signed off case files in 1 in 4 protection of vulnerable adults with learning disabilities case records we looked at.

Some social workers did not visit vulnerable adults with learning disabilities often enough. Social workers visited less than once a month in 1 in 3 cases of adults with learning disabilities who are at risk of abuse, neglect or exploitation. Other staff may have visited more often.

Scottish Borders Council and NHS Borders managers need to do more to weigh up the usefulness of training for professional practice.

Staff from all agencies should do more to support adults with learning disabilities to go to their own case conferences and reviews.

Joint records would help communication among agencies.

Good information which is up to date and jargon free would make a big difference to carers. Carers need practical help and support from professionals and carer support organisations. Professionals should understand carer's needs and see them as partners in care.

Some carers were not asked about important issues for the person they care for.

The Vulnerable Adults Protection Unit was not fully up and running. When it is, it should use this Borders follow up inspection report to write its work plan.

Education was not represented on the multi agency Adult Protection Committee. We think they should be.

People with learning disabilities were not represented on the Adult Protection Committee. We think they should be.

There has been a huge amount of work on the protection of vulnerable adults with learning disabilities. Can Scottish Borders Council, NHS Borders and their partners keep this up?

All of the national publications cited in this inspection report are available from the Scottish Executive website www.scotland.gov.uk

Methodology and Inspection Activities

Making the Borders Follow Up Inspection Happen

Scottish Borders Council, NHS Borders and their partners were outstandingly helpful and co-operative throughout the inspection. Without the excellent co-operation and support we got from all staff in Scottish Borders Council, NHS Borders and their partners, we could not have delivered this inspection. Scottish Borders Council appointed a full time staff member to work with the inspection team in the pre-inspection period and during the week of the inspection visit. NHS Borders identified a member of staff to be the contact person for the inspection. The two people worked exceptionally hard to make the inspection happen. Again, without their efforts we could not have delivered the inspection. We would like to thank all of the people with learning disabilities, family carers and members of staff who gave so freely of their time to make the inspection possible.

Verification Methodology

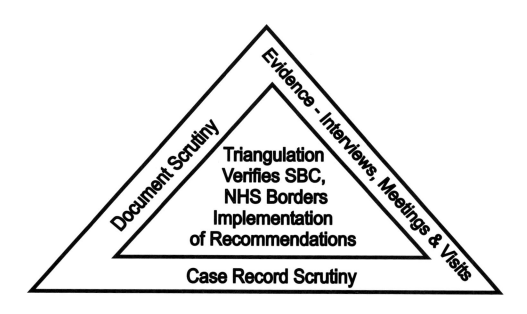

We tried to verify implementation of each of the Social Work Services Inspectorate and Mental Welfare Commission recommendations by Scottish Borders Council, NHS Borders and their partners. The above diagram shows the triangulation methodology we used. We applied three tests to each recommendation. Evidence of progress with implementation and work still to do, from:

- Documents provided;

- Case records scrutinised; and

- Interviews with people with learning disabilities, carers and staff and meetings and visits.

Scrutiny of case records

We asked Scottish Borders Social Work Department for a list of all adults and children with learning disabilities who are "allocated cases". We asked for information about closed cases. We chose a **random** selection of case records to scrutinise. We asked for case records as follows:

- Protection of vulnerable adults cases (50% of all cases requested for scrutiny);

- Adults with learning disabilities who have complex disabilities and high support needs;

- Non specific adults with learning disabilities cases;

- Young people with learning disabilities who are at the transition stage between services for children and services for adults; and

- Children with learning disabilities.

Scottish Borders Social Work Department provided over 90% of the cases we asked for. We scrutinised 61 social work case records.

We asked for all of the health records of people with learning disabilities who are subject to welfare guardianship (37 records). Staff from the Mental Welfare Commission scrutinised these records. They also looked at the social work records of people with learning disabilities on welfare guardianship.

We asked for the education records of a number of children with learning disabilities.

Date from which service improvements expected

We agreed with Scottish Borders Council and NHS Borders, that for the purposes of the record scrutiny, service improvements would be expected from **1 March 2003**. This is one year after the Borders abuse of the vulnerable adult case came to light. All the record scrutiny evidence that follows is based on what we found in the records from 1 March 2003.

Interviews with people with learning disabilities, family carers and staff

We chose a random sample of people with learning disabilities from the list provided by Scottish Borders social work department. Social Work asked these people if they would agree to be interviewed by an inspector. Most of the people agreed. The social work department and their partners made sure the people with learning disabilities got support before, during and after the interviews. The Scottish Consortium for Learning Disability and People First wrote the interview questions. We did individual interviews and a group interview.

We chose a random selection of family carers from the lists provided by social work. Family carers were asked if they would agree to be interviewed by an inspector. We did individual interviews and a group interview. Carers Scotland wrote the family carer interview questions.

We chose a random selection of staff (from all levels) from Scottish Borders Council and NHS Borders. We interviewed almost all of the staff initially selected. We interviewed staff individually and we held group sessions. We used standard questions for all of the staff interviews.

Scottish Borders Council's continuous improvement strategy and NHS Borders clinical governance plan

We do not want Scottish Borders Council and NHS Borders to write another action plan in response to this follow up inspection report. We agreed that they would incorporate work we identify as still to be done as part of Scottish Borders Council's continuous improvement strategy and NHS Borders' clinical governance process.

Other recommendations in the May 2004 Social Work Services Inspectorate and Mental Welfare Commission reports

SWSI recommendations 24 to 28 and Mental Welfare Commission recommendations 11 to 13 are for the Scottish Executive. Both reports recommend the Scottish Executive introduce a Vulnerable Adults Bill to complement existing statutory powers to protect vulnerable adults with learning disabilities and other vulnerable adults. Mental Welfare Commission recommendation 14 asks other regulators to take account of their report. The Scottish Executive will issue a statement, in due course, about progress implementing all of the foregoing recommendations.

Inspection Activities

The table below gives a summary of all of the things we did during the Borders follow up inspection.

Borders Follow Up Range of Inspection Activity
We interviewed 39 people with learning disabilities *(individual and group interviews and detailed survey done by Borders Independent Advocacy Service).*
We interviewed 17 family carers (individual and group interviews).
We interviewed over 40 staff from SBC and NHS Borders (individual and group interviews).
We scrutinised over 100 case records and records of supervision (social work, health, education).
We saw an additional 100 people with learning disabilities in large meetings.
We scrutinised over 200 documents.
We met with 10 representatives from the independent sector.
We met with 4 representatives from the local advocacy sector.
We participated in the SBC NHS Borders self assessment session.
We participated in the SBC NHS Borders good practice session.
We participated in the SBC Quality Services Network.
We participated in the SBC NHS Borders finance session.
We met the NHS Community Learning Disability Team and the Social Work Learning Disability Team *(scheduled to become joint team in September 2005).*
We met the Critical Oversight Scrutiny Group that oversees protection of vulnerable adults matters *(Chief Executives of Scottish Borders Council and NHS Borders and the Police Divisional Commander).*
We met the Adult Protection Committee including procurator fiscal and the area children's reporter.
We participated in the session on operational management of the protection of vulnerable adults.
We met with elected members including leader and deputy leader of the council.
We visited 2 GP practices.
We visited Borders General acute hospital.
We visited the out of hours service.
We visited a further education college.
We visited a special educational needs school.
We visited some children with learning disabilities in their homes.
There were concurrent inspections of regulated services by the Care Commission.

Progress delivering the Scottish Borders Council and NHS Borders Action Plan

This section sets out how Scottish Borders Council, NHS Borders and their partners are implementing the Social Work Services Inspectorate (SWSI) and the Mental Welfare Commission for Scotland recommendations, from their reports on the abuse of the vulnerable adults with learning disabilities who live in the Borders. The reports were published in May 2004.

SWSI Report Recommendation 1

> **The implementation of the recommendations contained in the Chief Social Work Inspector's letter to the Chief Executive of Scottish Borders Council dated 6 October 2003 should be continued.**

The Chief Social Work Inspector's letter is about the victims in the abuse of vulnerable adults with learning disabilities who live in Borders case. The letter is about:

- criminal injuries compensation applications for all the victims;

- independent legal representation for all individuals;

- independent advocacy for all individuals involved;

- current occupational and speech therapy assessments for some individuals;

- communication devices and their best use for some individuals; and

- contact that individuals wish to have with their relatives.

Scottish Borders Council and NHS Borders have fully implemented this recommendation.

SWSI Report Recommendation 2

> **Scottish Borders Council should consider making financial restitution to the individual concerned for these debts.**
> (The local authority failed to protect the finances of one individual to the extent that the person accrued some £3000 of debt whilst subject to guardianship).

Scottish Borders Council has implemented this recommendation.

SWSI Report Recommendation 3

> **Scottish Borders Council should review the implementation of its action plan for compliance as an employer with the Scottish Social Services Codes of Practice to ensure that it covers all the requirements of the Code and to ensure that implementation will secure the necessary changes in organisational behaviour described in this report, that are intended by the Code and that are essential to the effective functioning of the Department of Lifelong Care.**

Evidence of progress implementing SWSI recommendation 3

From scrutiny of documents

- Letters sent to all social work staff by Scottish Borders Council. Social work staff signed the letters acknowledging the Scottish Social Services Council (SSSC) Codes of Practice.

- Copies of social work job descriptions amended to comply with the SSSC Codes of Practice.

- An action plan on implementation of the Employers Codes of Practice approved by Council on 3 February 2004.

- A social work department training plan for 2004/2005, which addressed areas such as risk assessment, mental health, learning disabilities, the new management information system and supervisory skills.

- Management training including staff supervision, managing performance and Stirling University leadership training.

- Details of staff induction arrangements to Scottish Borders Council and the social work department.

- A copy of the review of the action plan.

From interviews with staff

During the inspection period **26** staff were interviewed individually. A further **84** staff were given questionnaires which sought their views on the effectiveness of the council's implementation of the Scottish Social Services Council Code of Practice. Only 20 survey forms were returned, all from social work.

We found social work staff were aware of the council's implementation of the Scottish Social Services Council Codes of Practice. Line managers provided staff with regular support and supervision. However we found no evidence that other staff (e.g. from education and housing) had a similar level of understanding.

Evidence of work still to be done

From scrutiny of documents

The review of the action plan noted delays in implementation which were due to workload pressures. The latest council recruitment information highlighted significant vacancies at supervisory level in adult services. In June 2005 there were three full time equivalent (FTE) senior social worker posts vacant, out of a staff complement of 11 FTE posts. There were 8.10 FTE social work posts vacant in adult services and 2.59 FTE occupational therapist posts (full staff complement for social workers 51.9 and for OTs 11.77).

The action plan focused on social work staff with little information about interagency or joint working.

From interviews with staff and questionnaire returns

We found no evidence of sampling or other methods to confirm that staff had an understanding of the Codes of Practice.

We found some evidence that training and development opportunities linked to the Codes of Practice.

Conclusion

Scottish Borders Council had ensured that staff who carry out social services tasks had been given information about the Codes of Practice. Almost all of them were aware of the codes and council policies to support the implementation of the codes. We found staff were uncertain about how these might work in practice. We found no evidence of other council services, including Education and Housing, being aware of their responsibilities.

SWSI Report Recommendation 4

> **The Department of Life Long Care should review the expertise of mental health officers operating in management positions and in all service areas to ensure they have up-to-date knowledge of relevant legislation, particularly as it relates to learning disability, issues of capacity and the protection of individuals and property. Without a more rigorous, formalised approach to the assumption of staffing expertise, this should not be relied upon for critical decision-making.**

Evidence of progress implementing recommendation 4

Evidence of progress from record scrutiny

The social work records were generally in good order. There was evidence of thorough assessments, co-operation with relevant agencies and careful attention given to the needs and feelings of people with learning disabilities and their families. This was most obvious in high-risk cases where protection of vulnerable adults procedures were used or where there were other statutory interventions, including Adults with Incapacity legislation or the use of the Mental Health Act.

From scrutiny of documents

The mental health officer (MHO) service had been reviewed by the social work department. A new post of team leader mental health was introduced. This manager had responsibility for overseeing the MHO Service and providing consultation, support and guidance to all practicing mental health officers, and the out of hours service. There were policies and procedures on the Mental Heath Act, Adults with Incapacity Act and the Protection of Vulnerable Adults in place.

The social work department created a new post of vulnerable adults protection co-ordinator to help improve the expertise of staff.

Social work staff completed training needs analysis and now have personal development plans. Details of the courses completed by MHOs were provided, and staff have taken part in a range of training courses to keep them up-to-date with new legislation and practice implications.

Four examples of MHOs' assessments were included as evidence. These assessments were comprehensive and included risk assessments. Decisions were made using good professional judgement.

From meetings and visits

The Director of Social Work Services examined all MHO portfolios and met with the candidates before they were accredited to practice in the Borders.

We found an increased focus on the protection of vulnerable adults in the Borders. There is a rise in the use of Welfare Guardianship.

From interviews with staff, people with learning disabilities and family carers

We found evidence of good multi-disciplinary working, with regular reviews of care plans. The learning disability consultant psychiatrist was regularly called upon to discuss complex cases, where there were issues of capacity and the protection of individuals. Quotes from mental health officers (MHOs).

> *"Feels like information overload but there is a need to record, justify decision making".*

> *"I have used the protection of vulnerable adults procedure several times, but only once to case conference. I am fully aware of the procedure".*

Evidence of work still to be done

From the scrutiny of records

The social work department should consider developing an audit tool on the use of mental health legislation and outcomes for people.

From scrutiny of documents

Not all MHOs have had recent specific training on working with people with learning disabilities.

From meetings and visits

The council need to agree who would have overall responsibility among existing managers for the management of complex cases. There was also a need to clarify where the role of vulnerable adult protection co-ordinator fitted into the existing structure.

From interviews with staff, people with learning disability and family carers

Personal development plans should ensure that social work staff and managers in all settings have up-to-date knowledge of relevant legislation, particularly as it relates to the protection of people with learning disabilities.

Conclusion

We found policies and procedures were in place, systems were being implemented and training opportunities provided. These should ensure that managers and MHOs have the expertise and up to date knowledge of relevant legislation to act appropriately when considering the protection of vulnerable adults with learning disabilities. Surveys of the impact of training and outcomes for individuals would provide further evidence of success in these areas.

SWSI Report Recommendation 5

> **Staff development programmes should include a focus on the complexities of adult protection; the role and thresholds for statutory intervention; and the duties that are extended and reinforced in the Adults with Incapacity and the Mental Health (Care and Treatment) Acts.**

Evidence of progress implementing recommendation 5

Evidence of progress from record scrutiny

Not applicable

From scrutiny of documents

A detailed and comprehensive joint NHS Borders and Scottish Borders Council Training Strategy had been written. This was being delivered to a wide range of staff. It was linked to continuous professional development.

The multi-agency vulnerable adults training programme, with 3 target levels, had been delivered to relevant staff:

- Awareness training targeted widely at all staff has been, to date, delivered to 1726 participants;

- Investigation to case conference, targeted to social work, health and police staff, has been delivered to 244 participants; and

- All team leaders had completed skill in chairing case conference training.

All MHOs were undertaking the transition course on the new Mental Health Act. A new joint funded training post would provide advice to health and social work staff on the requirements of the new legislation. Awareness sessions on the new act were also available to staff from all settings, including the independent sector and Borders General Hospital.

A specialist unit had been developed with the introduction of Adults with Incapacity (AWI) legislation. This provided social workers and their managers with consultation, guidance and support for their decision-making and practice skills. MHO's had also taken part in AWI training.

From meetings and visits

The multi-agency Adult Protection Committee was monitoring adult protection work.

A Scottish Borders Council and NHS Borders audit system ensured staff understood the complexities of adult protection work, and knew about policies and procedures.

The Joint Community Care Forum played an important role making sure training was provided to the independent sector, family carers and people with learning disabilities.

From interviews with staff, people with learning disabilities and family carers

Productive negotiations had taken place between the NHS and the local authority to develop a beacon site for training in Scottish Borders.

Staff had found the investigation to case conference course very helpful in clarifying roles and identifying thresholds for statutory intervention. All staff interviewed said that if they felt a person was at risk, they would contact their line manager in the first instance. Quotes from social workers:

> *"The training has got better and better".*

> *"If I thought a person with learning disabilities was at risk I would immediately inform my line manager or appropriate team leader. Involve health workers, police as necessary".*

Evidence of work still to be done

From scrutiny of documents

Managers should make sure, through effective supervision and audit, that all staff are doing mandatory training and know about the complexities of adult protection work.

The training courses on mental health legislation and the protection of vulnerable adults should be reviewed and evaluated frequently.

From interviews with staff, people with learning disabilities and family carers

Teams training needs analyses and individual training needs analysis should be regularly updated.

Conclusion

We found staff development programmes and standards were being developed to ensure a consistent approach to adult protection across Scottish Borders Council and NHS Borders. Consideration needed to be given to implementing multi-disciplinary training for all staff working with people with learning disabilities.

SWSI Report Recommendation 6

> **The Department of Life Long Care should develop a system of regular refresher training for mental health officers and should ensure that staff are aware how to access specialist advice and guidance, including legal advice.**

Evidence of progress implementing recommendation 6

Evidence of progress from record scrutiny

Not applicable.

From scrutiny of documents

The social work department had a mental health officer (MHO) training programme with regular refresher training. This was consistent with the accreditation requirements of the Mental Health Care and Treatment Act.

All MHOs had personal development plans which included personal training plans.

A Scottish Borders Council service level agreement for the provision of legal services to the social work department had been written. Legal services had increased the number of staff with knowledge and expertise in the area of mental health legislation to provide legal advice and action for MHOs. A customer satisfaction survey had recently been completed.

From meetings and visits

MHOs were participating in the continuing professional development programme provided by the South East of Scotland Training Consortium.

The mental health team and the adults with incapacity unit held surgeries in local social work offices.

A local multi-agency training forum delivered a range of training and seminars for staff.

From interviews with staff, people with learning disabilities and family carers

The mental health team leader led quarterly peer supervision for all MHOs who were not based in the mental health team. This was a new development which staff valued. A mental health officer said:

> *"I have been on both protection of vulnerable adults training courses and five day training on implementation of the new Mental Health Act. I have been to a conference on dual diagnosis. I am a member of the recovery network".*

> *"Supervision and scrutiny are necessary".*

Evidence of work still to be done

From scrutiny of documents

Any actions recommended following on from the review of work with legal services.

A review and evaluation of MHO refresher training should be considered.

From meetings and visits

A social work department review of the practice of all MHOs across all specialities was being planned. All MHOs should carry out the full range of MHO duties and have up to date knowledge and practice skills.

The social work department will need to consider how it will develop systems to monitor the use of National MHO Service Standards.

Conclusion

We found MHOs had the knowledge and practice skills to carry out their duties and responsibilities effectively.

The Department of Lifelong Care should carry out a review of all cases of adults with learning disabilities to assess the level of risk and determine the quality of service. The department should consider the level of seniority of staff conducting the review and may wish to commission the review from an independent source. The department should use a checklist for this review to ensure a consistent approach across all cases. The checklist should include (but not necessarily be restricted to) the following critical questions:

- Is there an allocated social worker with the necessary skills and experience to work with the complexities of this case?
- Has all the relevant information been gathered from departmental files, other departments, police, health and other involved sources?
- Is there a chronology of significant events and are the implications of these events understood?
- Is there a comprehensive assessment of risk and need?
- Is there evidence that the experiences of family members have been taken into account when assessing risk?
- Is there an appropriate care or protection plan that is being effectively implemented and that is demonstrably reducing the assessed risk?
- Has statutory intervention been considered and are the decisions in respect of this correct?
- Are copies of all minutes and records of decisions in the case file; have these been circulated to relevant individuals; and are the case records up-to-date?
- Is there evidence that the individual is being seen and spoken to on their own on a regular basis by the allocated social worker (where necessary using an interpreter or appropriate communication device); and have their living arrangements been seen?
- Is there evidence of good communication and collaboration between social work services, e.g. community care, criminal justice and children's services, and between social work and other key agencies, e.g. health, police, housing, education?
- Has the case been reviewed in accordance with procedure and has the individual been supported in contributing effectively to the review?
- Is there evidence that the social worker's handling of the case is subject to oversight by his/her line manager?

The results of the review, together with any proposals for remedial action, should be reported to elected members of the Council by the Chief Social Work Officer.

Evidence of progress implementing recommendation 7

Evidence of progress from record scrutiny

All social work case records scrutinised (n = 61)	Protection of vulnerable adults with learning disabilities social work cases (n = 20)
In 6 out of 61 records scrutinised there was no allocated social worker (see table in evidence of work still to be done section).	In all of the vulnerable adults cases scrutinised there was an allocated social worker.
72% of all records had important events highlighted.	85% of vulnerable adult records had important events highlighted.
74% of all records had an up to date risk assessment.	95% of vulnerable adults records had an up to date risk assessments.
77% of all records had a community care assessment or equivalent.	90% of vulnerable adults procedure records had a community care assessment or equivalent.
81% of all records were kept up to date.	90% of all vulnerable adults procedure records were kept up to date.
In 83% of all records there was evidence of effective multi agency joint working.	In 90% of vulnerable adult procedure cases there was evidence of effective multi agency joint working.
In 69% of all records there were regular case reviews.	In 80% of vulnerable adults procedure cases there were regular case reviews.
	95% of vulnerable adults procedure records had an up to date chronology of significant events.
	85% of vulnerable adults procedure records had a clear adult protection plan.
	In 95% of vulnerable adults procedure records there was evidence of good interagency communication about protection issues.
	In 95% of vulnerable adults procedure cases there was evidence of joint working to protect the person with learning disabilities.
	In 90% of cases the views of the person with learning disabilities informed the risk assessment.

	In 60% of vulnerable adult procedure cases scrutinised, statutory measures to protect the person with learning disabilities were considered. In 35% of vulnerable adult procedure cases scrutinised statutory measures were actually taken.
	In all of vulnerable adult procedure records, if statutory measures were considered but rejected, clear reasons were given for rejecting statutory measures.
	In only one case there was disagreement among multi-agency partners about not taking statutory measures to protect the person with learning disabilities.
	In 75% of cases the social worker regularly interviewed the person with learning disabilities on their own.
	In 95% of vulnerable adults procedure records the person with learning disabilities accommodation was seen and assessed for continued suitability.

Progress since social work's review of adults with learning disabilities cases April 2004

The social work department case audit tool and our file scrutiny template are different. We can make some useful comparisons between April 2004 and May 2005. The April 2005 report to Scottish Borders Council elected members said there were major problems with the standard of record keeping (based on the April 2004 audit).

Social work record issue	April 2004 position	May 2005 position
Up to date risk assessment	6.4%	74% (all cases)
Carers assessment	1.4%	28%
Key event summary	34.6% (all cases)	95% (protection vulnerable adults cases)
Protection of vulnerable adults case conference minutes in file	6.1% (all cases)	100% (protection of vulnerable adults cases)
Evidence of multi agency involvement	80. 9%	84% (all cases) 90% (PVA cases)
Prominent note of agencies & key staff	34%	86%

From document scrutiny

In April 2004, the social work department audited 381 adults with learning disabilities case files. Important findings from this audit are in the above table. Our May 2005 case record scrutiny shows evidence of significant progress in overall record keeping standards.

In January 2005 the social work department and NHS Borders did an audit of case records for "complex cases". Key findings were:

- None of 20 records audited showed evidence of people with learning disabilities being spoken to on their own; and

- In over 50% of cases no evidence of routine information sharing between professionals.

In December 2004 an independent consultant did an audit of protection of vulnerable adult cases. They found some good practice and some questionable practice.

In March 2005 the social work department did an audit of adult day services record keeping. Key findings were:

- Most support plans not fit for purpose;

- Huge variations in recording practice; and

- Some files very untidy and disorganised.

As a result of the adult day services recording audit there were now very clear written recording standards for adult day services.

The social work department had community care recording guidelines (December 2004) and social work case records policy, standards and guidance (no date). Both were comprehensive documents. These documents did not state how often team leaders/ managers should scrutinise and sign off case records.

There was a social work department staff supervision policy (November 2004). An appendix to this document states very clearly how often social work staff should be supervised.

From meetings

Staff present at the joint local authority, NHS finance meeting stated that the additional investment in services for people with learning disabilities was:

- Scottish Borders Council - £631.000 (05/06) for residential care services for adults with learning disabilities;

- Scottish Borders Council - £101.000 (05/06) for community care services for adults with learning disabilities;

- NHS Borders - £144.000 for implementation of the Scottish Borders Council NHS Borders action plan;

- NHS Borders - £450.000 for "complex cases"; and

- NHS Borders - £200.000 for young people with learning disabilities at the transition stage.

From staff interviews

All staff interviewed reported that recording was now a major priority. One social worker said:

> *"Writing things down is crucial. You have to evidence what you are doing".*

> *"In the past people recorded in all sorts of different ways, now we are all doing it the same way. It's easy to find information and not miss things".*

A number of staff however, said the need to keep accurate up to date records placed a big burden on them.

> *"I sometimes struggle to maintain the standard that is expected of me".*

There were some negative comments about the drive for better recording.

> *"Each case takes longer due to increased paper work and bureaucracy".*

> *"The amount of paperwork has quadrupled – has become more important than working with people".*

From interviews with people with learning disabilities and family carers

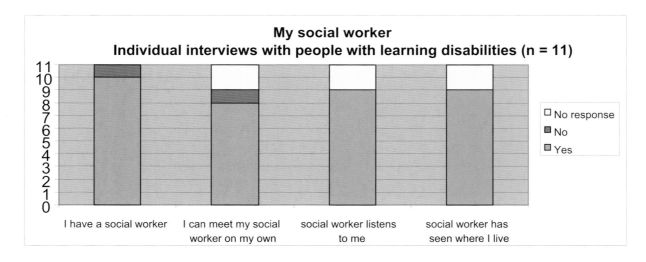

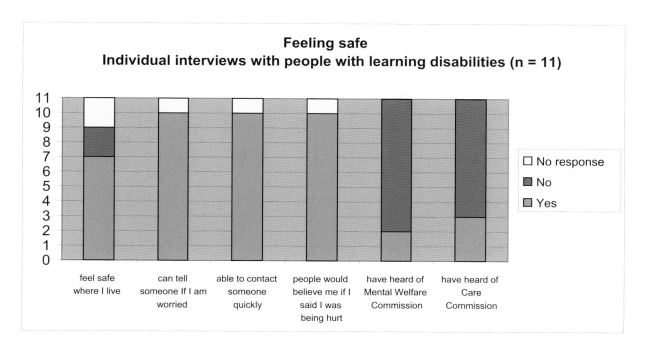

The above charts summarise what people with learning disabilities said about their social worker and about feeling safe.

Three of the 11 people with learning disabilities interviewed individually used an aid to communicate (picture and symbol board). One person said their communication aid was always used. Two people did not always have their communication aid available (for example at the interview with the inspector).

Most of the people with learning disabilities interviewed said:

- Their social worker listened to them;
- They would tell their social worker if something bad happened to them;
- Their social worker would act to protect them if asked to.

Care plans, personal life plans

The chart below summarises what people with learning disabilities said about care plans.

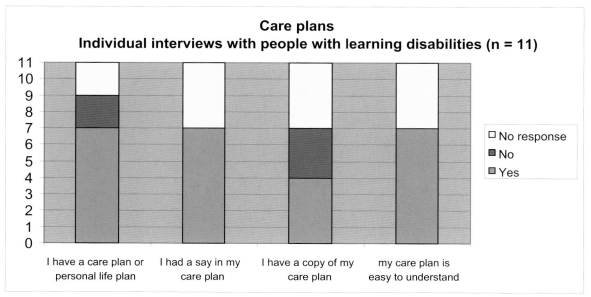

One person with learning disabilities said about their personal life plan:

"Yes is has pictures and is kept in the office. I can see it at any time".

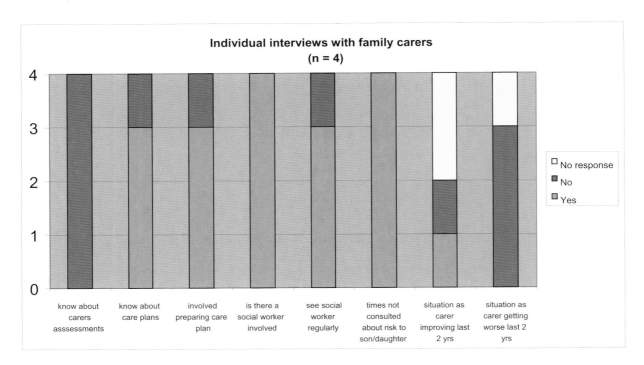

The above chart summarises the views of the family carers we interviewed.

One family carer said:

"I am very happy with the social worker".

One family carer who had not seen the social worker for twelve months said:

"I got very angry with the social worker as they didn't really know how my son was doing as they didn't ask".

Evidence of work still to be done

From record scrutiny

All social work case records scrutinised (n = 61)	Protection of vulnerable adults with learning disabilities social work cases (n = 20)
In 6 out of 61 records scrutinised there was no allocated social worker. In 4 of these unallocated cases we thought the case should have been allocated.	
51% of all records had a personal life plan or equivalent.	50% of all vulnerable adults procedure records had a personal life plan or equivalent.
54% of all records were regularly scrutinised by the line manager.	75% of all vulnerable adults procedure records were regularly scrutinised by the line manager.
In 59% of all records the person with learning disabilities was seen by the social worker/care manager less than once a month. 30% were seen between fortnightly and monthly. Only 11% were seen more than once a fortnight.	In 15% of vulnerable adult procedure records the person with learning disabilities was seen more than once a fortnight, 55% were seen between fortnightly and monthly, 30% were seen less than once a month.

In some cases, it appeared that records had been scrutinised. There were initials next to entries in the record that were clearly not those of the allocated social worker. It was often difficult to tell whose initials they were.

Conclusion

The social work department had done a number detailed audits of case records. There had been a huge drive to improve the quality of social work recording. Our May 2005 audit showed a significant improvement in the quality of recording since the April 2004 internal audit. We found problems with some line managers scrutinising and signing off case records. We were concerned, that in nearly a third (30%) of protection of vulnerable adults cases the social worker saw the person with learning disabilities less than once a month.

SWSI Report Recommendation 8

> **All allegations of harm or neglect of people with learning disabilities should be allocated to a social worker. Managers allocating cases must be clear as to what has been allocated, what action is required and how those actions will be reviewed and supervised. Supervision arrangements should include formal case management, with all decisions clearly recorded by the supervisor and monitored at regular intervals.**

Evidence of progress implementing recommendation 8

Evidence of progress from record scrutiny

Protection of vulnerable adult with LD social work cases where there was specific harm or neglect allegations (n = 8)	All protection of vulnerable adult with learning disabilities social work cases (n = 20)
All 8 cases had an allocated social worker.	100% of vulnerable adult cases had an allocated social worker.
In all 8 cases, the investigating social workers were clear about the purpose of any proposed visit or investigation.	In 95% of cases, the Council's Protection of Vulnerable Adults Procedure had been applied.
In all 8 cases, the investigating social workers were clear what information they should gather.	In 85% of cases, records included a clear adult protection plan.
	In 80% of cases, the case had been reviewed at appropriate intervals. Also there was a clear mechanism for checking whether action points were being delivered in practice.
	In 95% of cases, we found evidence that the person with learning disabilities was protected. *(We told the social work department about the one case where we felt the person with learning disabilities was not adequately protected. They have addressed the issues).*

From scrutiny of documents

The Social Work Community Care Manual: Protection of Vulnerable Adults stated '... the first task ...(of the locality manager)... will be the appointment of an investigating officer to the case. Normally, this officer will be the social worker most familiar with the case (paragraph 4)".

The manual went on to say that an action plan would be written at an initial stage, after discussion between the social work staff member taking the referral and the line manager. The vulnerable adult protection investigation record set out a requirement for outcomes, persons responsible and timescales to be clearly recorded at initial, full and review stages of any investigation.

The Social Work Services Supervision Policy (November 2004) stated '…an expectation that all open cases will formally be reviewed annually.' (paragraph 4e).

Scottish Borders Council recently brought in an external practice adviser to do a protection of vulnerable adults case audit. In early 2005 the external practice adviser reviewed nine protection of vulnerable adults cases. They then made recommendations to the council.

From meetings and visits

Our meetings with practitioners and representatives from the independent sector revealed they were well aware of protection of vulnerable adults procedures. In all meetings, there was a general view that systems to protect vulnerable adults had improved.

From interviews with staff, people with learning disabilities and family carers

We found widespread knowledge and understanding of the protection of vulnerable adults procedure amongst all staff. Some comments from staff:

> *"Vulnerable adults guidelines are on the intranet. We all have access to paper copies in local offices and in our desks. They are always to hand" (social worker).*

> *"Vulnerable adults policy is helpful, clear procedure and who to contact" (NHS primary care staff).*

Evidence of work still to be done

From record scrutiny

Impact from supervision sessions carried out by line managers with social workers registered in only 30% of protection of vulnerable adults cases (n=20).
From the small number of staff supervision records examined (n=6), there was evidence of supervision being carried out on a regular basis. However, supervision records rarely stated whether previous action points had been carried out. There was no means of clearly identifying protection issues for vulnerable adults in the supervision record. Changes to the supervision record template would quickly rectify these issues.
In 75% of protection of vulnerable adults cases there was evidence that the first line manager regularly scrutinised the file (n=20).

We identified a person on Welfare Guardianship who did not have an allocated social worker for a year. One health professional had regular contact with the person. That professional's health records contained no information about the powers of the Welfare Guardian or the risks to the person's welfare. The new team leader discovered the problem and took immediate action to make sure that the person was protected. This case was included in the social work department's audit, but no mention was made of this gap in care.

From scrutiny of documents

Neither the Social Work Community Care Recording Guidelines (December 2004), nor the Social Work Services Supervision Policy (November 2004) explicitly set out how decisions reached in supervision should be recorded on the case file.

From interviews with staff, people with learning disabilities and family carers

No significant concerns were raised in the course of individual interviews.

Conclusion

We found the profile of vulnerable adults with learning disabilities and their right to effective protection was being given sufficient priority by Scottish Borders Council and its partners. We found staff knew about the steps needed to protect vulnerable adults with learning disabilities. We found significant improvement in standards of social work practice. This was evident in case records.

Whilst clear progress had been made in supporting and monitoring practice, more effort is required to improve quality assurance. Once set up the vulnerable adults protection unit will help with this. This would complement the monitoring done by line managers.

SWSI Report Recommendation 9

> **People with learning disabilities who are the subject of allegations of deliberate harm (regardless of the source of the allegations) must be seen and spoken to alone or with the appropriate support within 24 hours of the allegations being communicated to social work. The individual's living arrangements should be seen. If this time scale is not met, the reason for the failure must be recorded on the case file. This requirement should apply irrespective of whether the case is known to the department.**

Evidence of progress implementing recommendation 9

Evidence of progress from record scrutiny

Protection of vulnerable adult with learning disabilities social work cases where there is specific harm or neglect allegation (n = 8)
The person's living arrangements were seen in all 8 investigations.
In 7 out of 8 cases, investigating workers spoke with the person with learning disabilities on their own or with appropriate support.

From scrutiny of documents

The Social Work Community Care Manual: Protection of Vulnerable Adults procedure set the standard – i.e. that 'There should be face to face contact with the vulnerable adult alone or with support, within 24 hours of the allegation being made.' The manual also requires an assessment of the vulnerable adult's living circumstances.

From meetings and visits

No significant issues were raised in the course of meetings and visits.

From interviews with staff, people with learning disabilities and family carers

One social worker said:

> *"The profile of protection of vulnerable adults is much higher within the social work department. All case records are being audited by line managers and sampled by senior managers. Team leaders randomly pick files to examine at supervision".*

Eight out of 11 people with learning disabilities interviewed individually felt able to see their social worker on their own.

Nine out of 11 people with learning disabilities interviewed individually said their social worker had seen where they live.

Evidence of work still to be done

Protection of vulnerable adults with learning disabilities social work cases where there is a specific harm or neglect allegation (n = 8)
In 5 out of 8 cases the social worker saw the person with learning disabilities within 24 hours. In the 3 cases where the person was not seen within this period the reason for delay was recorded in only one instance.

From scrutiny of documents

The vulnerable adult protection investigation record did not include any of the following:

- The date when the vulnerable adult was seen alone or with appropriate support;

- The date on which an assessment of the vulnerable adult's living circumstances was carried out; and

- Reasons for not being able to carry out either of the above tasks.

For monitoring purposes, it would be helpful if this information was added to the investigation record.

From meeting and visits

No significant concerns were raised in the course of meetings and visits.

From interviews with staff, people with learning disabilities and family carers

No significant concerns were raised during interviews with staff, people with learning disabilities and family carers.

Conclusion

As recommendation 8.

SWSI Report Recommendation 10

> In cases where concerns have been expressed about the safety of a person with learning disabilities (regardless of source), social workers undertaking home visits should be clear about the purpose of the visit, the information to be gathered during the course of it, and the steps to be taken if no one is at home or if access is denied. No visits should be undertaken without the social worker concerned checking the information known about the individual by other agencies.

Evidence of progress implementing recommendation 10

Evidence of progress from record scrutiny

Protection vulnerable adult with LD social work cases where there is specific harm or neglect allegation (n = 8)	All protection of vulnerable adult with learning disabilities social work cases (n = 20)
In all 8 cases, the investigating social workers were clear about the purpose of any proposed visit or investigation.	In 95% of cases, there was evidence of good inter agency communication about protection issues.
In all 8 cases, the investigating social workers were clear what information to gather.	In 95% of cases, there was evidence of joint work to protect the person with learning disabilities.
	There was a prominent note of all involved agencies and key staff in 95% of case files. Clear contact details for key agencies and key staff were kept in 95% of case files.
	In 95% of cases, there was evidence of joint work to protect the person with learning disabilities.

From scrutiny of documents

There had been a wide protection of vulnerable adults training programme. There were 1726 participants from partner agencies. In addition, 244 staff from police, the NHS and social work had undertaken more intensive investigation to case conference vulnerable adults training. In general the feedback was very positive.

From interviews with staff, people with learning disabilities and family carers

Staff interviewed knew all about the protection of vulnerable adults procedure, its purpose and the expectations it placed upon individual staff. The extensive training programme (see above) was often referred to. A nurse said:

"The protection of vulnerable adults procedures are very client focussed. They are not overprotective. Glad the protection of vulnerable adult procedures are in place, as they are a safety net for all concerned".

In addition, links between agencies were generally seen as much improved. Operational links between social work and community psychiatric and learning disability nursing received specific mention. A social worker said:

"There is much more awareness of inter – agency working now".

Evidence of work still to be done

From record scrutiny

Protection of vulnerable adult with learning disabilities social work cases where there is specific harm or neglect allegation (n = 8)
In 6 out of 8 cases where there was a specific harm or neglect allegation, there was evidence that social workers checked with other agencies for relevant information.

From scrutiny of documents

The Social Work Community Care Manual: Protection of Vulnerable Adults does not explicitly refer to the issue of what to do in the event of no one being at home or if access is denied, other than to record the fact.

From meetings, visits

We could not tell if the extensive protection of vulnerable adults training programme had reached community education and further education college staff.

From interviews with staff, people with learning disabilities and family carers

No significant concerns were raised in the course of individual interviews.

Conclusion

As recommendation 8.

SWSI Report Recommendation 11

All allegations of harm or neglect of people with learning disabilities must be subject to a risk assessment. All risk assessments, and any protection plans drawn up as a result, must be approved in writing by the social worker's line manager. Before giving such approval, the line manager must ensure that the individual has been seen and spoken to alone or with appropriate support. A senior manager should routinely consider a random sample of risk assessments and associated protection plans.

Evidence of progress implementing recommendation 11

Evidence of progress from record scrutiny

Protection of vulnerable adult with LD social work cases where there is specific harm or neglect allegation (n = 8)	All protection of vulnerable adult with learning disabilities social work cases (n = 20)
See all VA cases column	95% of cases had up to date risk assessment.
See all VA cases column	In 90% of cases views of people with learning disabilities informed the risk assessment.
See all VA cases column	In 95% of cases, Scottish Borders Council's partners informed the risk assessment. In one case partners' views did not inform the risk assessment.
See all VA cases column	In 95% of relevant cases family & other views informed the risk assessment. (not applicable in 30% of cases as no family carer involved).
In 7 out of 8 cases, investigating workers spoke with the person with learning disabilities on their own or with appropriate support.	In 75% of cases, the social worker regularly interviewed the person with learning disabilities on their own.

From scrutiny of documents

All of the policy and procedure documents examined said all of the points in recommendation 11 should be actioned by relevant staff.

From meetings and visits

Evidence from meetings was that recommendation 11 was being implemented. Inspectors who visited the out of hours service found they had risk assessment forms.

Most of the staff we interviewed had done some risk assessment training. All staff interviewed knew about the need for risk assessments for people with learning disabilities. Staff spoke about a risk assessment tool being incorporated into the single shared assessment procedures for people with learning disabilities. These procedures were only just being put in place. Some comments from staff:

> _"There is much more conscious effort to carry out risk management"._

> _"The social work department is the pilot for the risk assessment/risk management process- mainly use of risk matrix to identify effective controls"._

Evidence of work still to be done

From record scrutiny

All protection of vulnerable adult with learning disabilities social work cases (n = 20)
In only 10% of vulnerable adults cases scrutinised was there evidence that a senior manager had examined the file i.e. no evidence of scrutiny by any senior manager in 90% of cases. NB this is in the period 1 March 2003 to 1 May 2005.
In 75% of cases, a team leader regularly examined and signed off the file. Thus in 25% of vulnerable adults cases the file was not regularly examined and signed off by a team leader or other manager.
In 25% of vulnerable adults cases the person with learning disabilities was not regularly seen on their own.

From scrutiny of documents

There was only passing mention of risk assessment in the Protection of Vulnerable Adults Procedure. It would be helpful if the risk assessment tool was in the appendices. Documents said that an inter agency steering group was monitoring practice in this area. Other evidence was that participation in this group was poor (four representatives) with the NHS and the police not represented. The capacity of this group to monitor compliance with recommendation 11 was therefore questionable.

From meetings and visits

The Scottish Borders Council and NHS Borders action plan stated, (from September 2004) the vulnerable adults protection unit would monitor compliance with this recommendation. From our meetings with Scottish Borders Council and NHS Borders it was clear that at the beginning of May 2005 they were still setting up the vulnerable adults protection unit. The unit co-ordinator was appointed at the beginning of May 2005 and they were recruiting other staff.

From interviews with staff, people with learning disabilities and family carers

One staff member commented that there was not enough guidance on using the new risk assessment procedures.

One staff member commented:

> _"Poor information sharing between the local authority and the NHS is hampering effective risk assessment of people with learning disabilities"._

All four of the family carers we interviewed individually said they had not been consulted about some risk issues for their sons and daughters. Some of the family carers involved in the group interview session said they had not been consulted about some risk issues.

Conclusion

We found good progress implementing this recommendation. Line management scrutiny was greatly improved however, senior managers needed to sample and scrutinise more case records.

SWSI Report Recommendation 12

> **The accommodation and living arrangements of any individual subject of allegations of abuse must be monitored and reviewed by the allocated social worker. Unsuitable arrangements must be reported to a line manager.**

Evidence of progress implementing recommendation 12

Evidence of progress from record scrutiny

Protection of vulnerable adult with LD social work cases where there is specific harm or neglect allegation (n = 8)	All protection of vulnerable adult with learning disabilities social work cases (n = 20)
In all 8 cases the investigating social worker(s) saw the person with learning disabilities living arrangements.	In 90% of cases social work assessed the person with learning disabilities accommodation for continued suitability.

From scrutiny of documents

All Scottish Borders Council and NHS Borders policy and procedure documents we examined clearly stated that all of the points in recommendation 12 should be actioned by relevant staff.

A copy of the new social work referral form was provided. It had sections on assessment of accommodation.

From interviews with staff, people with learning disabilities and family carers

Staff said that the range and amount of training had increased recently and new policies and procedures had been introduced.

Of the 11 people with learning disabilities interviewed, 9 stated that their social worker had seen where they lived and only 2 said they had not.

Conclusion

We found structures and processes to ensure this recommendation is implemented and monitored.

SWSI Report Recommendation 13

All case conferences, case reviews, meetings and discussions concerning people with learning disabilities should involve the four basic steps:

- **A list of action points must be drawn up, each with an agreed timescale and the identity of the person responsible for carrying it out;**
- **A clear record of the discussion must be circulated to all those invited, whether or not they were present, and to all those with responsibility for an action point;**
- **A mechanism for reviewing completion of the agreed actions must be specified, together with the date upon which the first such review is to take place; and**
- **Any supplementary actions that may be required as a contingency in the event of a breakdown in care arrangements or other changes in circumstances.**

Evidence of progress implementing recommendation 13

Evidence of progress from record scrutiny

All protection of vulnerable adult with learning disabilities social work cases (n = 20)
100% of vulnerable adult case records had minutes of case conferences and review meetings in the file.
90% of records had case conference minutes with clear lists of action points.
90% of records had case conference minutes that state who is responsible for carrying out the action points.
In 80% of records it was clear that case conference minutes were sent out to all those invited to the conference even if they did not attend.
In 77% of records family carers were invited to attend case conferences and reviews.

From document scrutiny

The undated unsigned social work department practice standards statement set out SWSI recommendation 13 and said that it should be complied with.

From interviews with staff

One social work team leader said:

> *"I have attended twenty (protection of vulnerable adults with learning disabilities) case conferences in last 7 months. There has been a huge increase in referrals since awareness was raised".*

Evidence of work still to be done

From record scrutiny

All protection of vulnerable adult with learning disabilities social work cases (n = 20)
In 30% of case records the person with learning disabilities was not invited to attend case conferences and reviews.
In 50% of case records the person with learning disabilities did not attend case conferences and reviews.
In 40% of records case conference and review minutes did not have clear timescales for carrying out agreed actions.
In 45% of records family carers did not attend case conferences and reviews (although in some cases it may not have been appropriate for them to do so).

On action points and timescales for action, we found further evidence from the scrutiny of staff supervision notes. In all six of the staff supervision notes scrutinised there were issues with action points, timescales for action and making sure actions were done. Issues were:

- Some supervision notes had no clear timescales for action;

- There was no system for checking if agreed actions had in fact been done; and

- No explicit links between action points and the care plan/adult protection plan.

We found practice was inconsistent across partner agencies. Evidence from children and young people's education and psychological service files suggested that the four basic steps (from recommendation 13) were not yet embedded in practice. All agencies should ensure that case conferences, case reviews, meetings and discussion concerning people with learning disabilities meet the recording standards outlined in recommendation 13. It would be helpful to develop a Borders wide protocol for all people with learning disabilities which would link to the new Additional Support for Learning legislation.

From document scrutiny

A number of protection of vulnerable adults case conference minutes were sent as documentary evidence. This was in addition to those examined with protection of vulnerable adults case records. Few of the minutes supplied had clear target dates and timescales for actions. There was evidence from some case conference minutes of identifying supplementary actions that may be required as a contingency in the event of a breakdown in care arrangements or other changes in circumstances.

Conclusion

We found some good progress implementing this recommendation. More needed to be done to encourage and support people with learning disabilities to attend their case conferences and review meetings. The social work department need to ensure that required actions are done to agreed timescales.

SWSI Report Recommendation 14

> The interview of people with learning disabilities subject to alleged abuse should be formally planned. Planning should include consideration of a safe environment; the use of interviewers with the necessary skills and understanding; the emotional support needs of the individual; and the use of necessary communication aids or an interpreter. The interview should be recorded in detail, using the individual's own words.

Evidence of progress implementing recommendation 14

Evidence of progress from record scrutiny

Protection of vulnerable adult with learning disabilities social work cases where there is specific harm or neglect allegation (n = 8)
In 5 out of 8 cases, the investigating social workers formally planned their interview with the person with learning disabilities.
In all 8 cases the investigating social workers were clear about the information they were to gather.
In 7 out of 8 cases the investigating social workers spoke with the person with learning disabilities alone or with appropriate support.

From scrutiny of documents

We found clear evidence of training in interview skills. This contributed to the protection of vulnerable adults through procedure, policy and practice.

Joint training in interviewing (*investigation of vulnerable adults abuse to case conference*) had been delivered to 244 staff from NHS Borders, Scottish Borders Council and Lothian and Borders Police. The training materials were of a good standard. We found staff liked the training.

A small scale and limited audit of health and social work staff training highlighted gaps in knowledge and the number of staff still awaiting training (Approximately 50%).

Awareness level vulnerable adult protection was included in the NHS Borders organisational induction course for new members of staff. This course was run every month and is delivered over 2 days for clinical staff (1.5 days for non clinical).

From interviews with staff, people with learning disabilities and family carers

A social worker working in the out of hours service said about training:

> *"Responsive with good police links and working relationships".*

> *"I found the interview training very helpful". (social worker, community care team).*

"Joint training has given people more confidence and has encouraged communication between social workers, health care staff and the police". (social worker, out of hours service).

Evidence of work still to be done

From record scrutiny

Protection of vulnerable adult with learning disabilities social work cases where there is specific harm or neglect allegation (n = 8)
In 3 out of 8 cases the investigating social workers recorded the interview in detail in the person with learning disabilities own words.

From scrutiny of documents

The effectiveness of interview training needs to be evaluated. We could not tell how much staff knowledge, understanding and practice is changed because of the training. A systematic audit of interview training is needed.

We were not clear on whether the timetable for training staff on the *"rolling programme"* of training would be completed. Similarly, the number of appropriate adults taking up interview training needs to be carefully monitored.

From meetings and visits

A number of independent sector staff who were supporting vulnerable people with learning disabilities had been offered, but had not taken up any interview or awareness training. This was a significant omission given the number of independent sector staff working directly with adults with learning disabilities.

All GPs were invited to the training. No GP had taken up the offer of training.

Conclusion

We found good progress implementing this recommendation. Training needed to be provided to staff from all organisations who work with people with learning disabilities in the Borders.

SWSI Report Recommendation 15

> **The Department of Lifelong Care should ensure that where the investigation of allegations of abuse may be impeded by the threat of violence to staff, staff are effectively protected and supported in carrying out their task. This should include visits being carried out in pairs, or involvement of the police where appropriate.**

Evidence of progress implementing recommendation 15

Evidence of progress from record scrutiny

All protection of vulnerable adult with learning disabilities social work cases (n = 20)
There were concerns about violence to staff in 25% of the protection of vulnerable adult cases. Effective steps were taken to protect staff in **all** of these cases.

From scrutiny of documents

A social work department lone working policy and a risk assessment system was to be used to identify those staff who required mobile phones.

Social work training plans included risk assessment and risk management.

From meetings and visits

We found social work staff had more training opportunities, including risk assessment and leadership.

From interviews with staff, people with learning disabilities and family carers

Staff in the emergency duty team were aware of the lone working policy and confirmed its implementation.

Mobile phones had been provided to some staff and the emergency team members always went out in pairs, either with the police or with another colleague.

We found good evidence of increased multi-agency working and support and leadership from line managers. One member of staff said, *"people not so precious about roles"*.

Individual staff interviewed said that leadership and communication between front line staff and managers had improved.

Evidence of work still to be done

From scrutiny of documents

Details of the management information systems developed to monitor violence to staff issues were not available. Audit outcomes were not available.

From interviews with staff, people with learning disabilities and family carers

The glut of new information could hinder communication. One staff member said:

> *"There is no shared record keeping, we sometimes have information overload".*

Conclusion

We found structures and processes were in place. The outcomes required to be audited.

SWSI Report Recommendation 16

The Department of Lifelong Care should devise and operate a system that enables managers to establish immediately how many vulnerable people have been referred to their out of hours service, what action is required for each referral, who is responsible for taking that action, and by when that action must be completed.

Evidence of progress implementing recommendation 16

Evidence of progress from record scrutiny

All protection of vulnerable adults with learning disabilities social work cases (n = 20)
95% of case records had prominent note of agencies involved, key staff and contact details.
90% of case records had minutes with clear lists of action points.
95% of case records had an up to date chronology of key events.

From scrutiny of documents

Scottish Borders Council had a Critical Information Exchange Protocol. The social work department gave us details of out of hours activity relating to the protection of vulnerable adults.

A basic database of all referrals to the out of hours team was provided.

From meetings and visits

A social work emergency duty team provided out of hours services every day. They were a highly motivated group of staff. They had developed good links and relationships with other agencies including the police.

We found good transfer of information between "office hours" services and the out of hours service. Out of hours staff said a list of vulnerable adults at risk is part of the record keeping system.

From interviews with staff, people with learning disabilities and family carers

An NHS primary care staff member said:

> " Recent (protection of vulnerable adult) case at the weekend.
> Contacted Border Care and the social work out of hours team.
> Policy indicated case conference. Action taken within 24 hours".

Evidence of work still to be done

From scrutiny of documents

The electronic database was basic and was not immediately available to all.

From meetings and visits

Accommodation for the out of hour's team was cramped and was shared by three other groups.

There were plans to develop a linked database between the NHS and Scottish Borders Council. We found no joint records at the time of the inspection.

There was a protocol for sharing information for the Scottish Borders Council team but none as yet for the NHS. A joint protocol was available but we found this was not sufficiently detailed or operational.

Conclusion

We found a system to enable compliance with this recommendation.

SWSI Report Recommendation 17

> **The Department of Lifelong Care should ensure that their senior managers inspect, at least once every three months, a random selection of case files and staff supervision notes.**

Evidence of work still to be done

From record scrutiny

Case type	Social work records	Is there evidence that senior managers periodically scrutinise the file	Is the impact of worker supervision sessions evident in the case record
Protection of vulnerable adult with LD cases	n=20	Yes in 10% of cases	Yes in 30% of cases
Adults with learning disabilities general cases	n=21	Yes in 10% of cases	Yes in 24% of cases
Adults with LD complex disabilities	n=10	Yes in 4 cases	Yes in 3 cases
Transition cases	n=8	Yes in 0 cases	Yes in 0 cases
Children with learning disabilities	n=2	Yes in 0 cases	Yes in 0 cases
All cases	n=61	Yes in 13% of cases	Yes in 23% of cases

Senior managers scrutinised 13% of all social work learning disability case records. Paradoxically the rate of scrutiny by senior managers was less for protection of vulnerable adults cases than for all learning disability cases.

We were concerned about the low proportion of protection of vulnerable adults case records scrutinised by senior managers. There was a procedure for senior managers to scrutinise case records annually. This had been changed to scrutiny every three months. We found little evidence this was happening. Senior managers inspected only one in ten protection of vulnerable adults cases. The current rate of senior manager inspection of these cases means senior managers inspected one protection of vulnerable adult case record every three months (assuming protection of vulnerable adults cases are subject of the protection of vulnerable adults procedure for a mean period of one year and senior managers inspected a different case record every three months).

The impact of worker supervision sessions was evident in fewer than one in four case files.

We found senior managers had inspected none of the six social work staff supervision records scrutinised.

We found 54% of all social work files had been scrutinised and signed off by *line* managers. There were however, some very positive comments about this process from staff:

> *"All case records are being audited by line managers and sampled by senior managers. Team leaders randomly pick files to examine at supervision." (social worker, community care team).*

> *"More effective audit and supervision of staff; role modelling the behaviours the department expects of all staff. There are formal systems – supervision linked to case recording." (group manager, community care).*

From scrutiny of documents

We found no evidence of outcomes of senior managers "*shadowing*" of staff on home visits to people with learning disabilities.

Conclusion

Senior managers should inspect more protection of vulnerable adults with learning disabilities case files, more often. They should inspect more staff supervision notes more often. Staff supervision should be recorded appropriately in case files. The social work department should specify the:

- numbers of all learning disability case files senior managers should scrutinise;

- numbers of protection of vulnerable adults with learning disabilities case files senior managers should scrutinise; and

- numbers of staff supervision notes senior managers should scrutinise.

SWSI Report Recommendation 18

> **The Department of Lifelong Care should monitor the effective implementation of its procedures relating to the transfer of cases between teams or services within the department.**

Evidence of progress implementing recommendation 18

Evidence of progress from record scrutiny

See the table in work still to be done.

From document scrutiny

There was a social work department case transfer procedure in place. This had a transfer summary form. This required to be signed off by the team leader. Transfer summaries and arrangements were included in the current social work case record auditing procedures. Transfer summaries and arrangements were not included in the social work department's April 2004 audit of adults with learning disabilities case records.

There were education authority transition procedures in place for children and young people transferring from primary to secondary education, and from secondary to further education placements.

In April 2005, a draft protocol was developed for the transition from children to adult services for young people with a disability (Report on Multi-Agency Procedures for Transition from Children to Adult Services for Young People with a Disability). The protocol was developed by a number of agencies. However, there was no representation from schools or community learning and development. It would be helpful if the education representation could be increased, as the only educational representative at present is the educational psychologist. The protocol focused on professional needs, rather than the outcomes and impact for people with learning disabilities.

Evidence of work still to be done

From record scrutiny

Case type	Social work records	Evidence from social work record scrutiny on transfer arrangements
Protection of vulnerable adult with LD social work cases	(n = 8)	4 relevant case records sampled (case transferred) did not have appropriate transfer summaries.
Adults with learning disabilities general cases	(n =10)	70% of the relevant cases sampled did not have appropriate transfer summaries.
Adults with LD complex disabilities	(n = 3)	2 of the relevant cases sampled did not have appropriate transfer summaries.
Transition cases	(n = 3)	2 of the relevant cases sampled did not have appropriate transfer summaries.
Children with learning disabilities		None of the case records sampled required transfer summaries.
All cases	(n = 24)	62% of relevant cases did not have appropriate transfer summaries.

Further work on joint planning and information sharing was required between agencies and partners. We could not always tell from the education and educational psychology files what services were expected from education and partner agencies. Greater case and file co-ordination was required.

From document scrutiny

There were no formal procedures in place for transition in the early years. These procedures were developed by education and now needed to be formalised to ensure that all children and young people had access to the same high quality planning at transition. Further work was required to ensure that the procedures were extended to other agencies.

Conclusion

We found limited progress with Scottish Borders Councils implementation of this recommendation. More work was needed on arrangements for transfer of cases and succinct transfer summaries. More requires to be done to ensure that the needs of people with learning disabilities and family carers are met consistently through any transition stage.

SWSI Report Recommendation 19

> The Department of Lifelong Care should ensure that no open case that includes allegations of deliberate harm to a vulnerable adult is closed until the following steps have been taken:
>
> - The individual has been spoken to alone;
> - The individual's accommodation has been visited;
> - The views of all relevant professionals have been sought and considered; and
> - There is evidence that the individual's welfare will be safeguarded and promoted should the case be closed.

Evidence of progress implementing recommendation 19

Evidence of progress from record scrutiny

All protection of vulnerable adult with learning disabilities social work cases (n = 20)
In 75% of cases, the social worker regularly interviewed the person with learning disabilities on their own.
There was evidence of effective multi-agency joint working in 90% of cases.
There was evidence of good inter agency communication about protection issues in 95% of cases.
The service had assessed the person with learning disabilities accommodation for continued suitability in 95% of cases.

From scrutiny of documents

The Social Work Community Care Manual: Protection of Vulnerable Adults stated that '… A case involving adult abuse should not be closed without there being discussion with the vulnerable adult and a re-assessment of their living circumstances being undertaken. All key professionals should be consulted and be in agreement with the intention to close the case.' (Paragraph 10).

From meetings and visits

No significant issues were raised regarding case closure in the course of meetings and visits.

From interviews with staff, people with learning disabilities and family carers

Staff interviewed knew about the need to liaise closely at each stage of assessment, planning and at the point of closure. Staff interviewed were clear about how to resolve areas of disagreement. No-one we interviewed had found it necessary to invoke the inter-agency protocol. One NHS staff member said that if there was a dispute with a colleague in a protection of vulnerable adults case they would:

> "Discuss with the person then the line manager. Helpful to have the Dispute Resolution Protocol there – never used it".

Evidence of work still to be done

From record scrutiny

In 25% of vulnerable adults cases the person with learning disabilities was not regularly seen on their own.
Of the 4 case closures examined, we thought **3 were satisfactory**.

From scrutiny of documents

The Social Work Community Care Manual: Protection of Vulnerable Adults needed to be more specific in order to meet this recommendation.

- It should be explicit that the vulnerable adult must be seen alone at the point the case is closed, with appropriate support if necessary; and

- Evidence that the person's future welfare will continue to be safeguarded and promoted should be clearly entered on the closure summary and kept in the case record.

Scottish Borders Council and NHS Borders submitted a document called "Process To Be Utilised When There Is A Disagreement Between Agencies Over How To Proceed With The Care Of An Individual". The exact status of this document was unclear as it was not signed or dated.

From meetings and visits

No significant issues were raised regarding case closure in course of meetings and visits.

From interviews with staff, people with learning disabilities and family carers

No significant concerns were raised in the course of individual interviews.

Conclusion

As recommendation 8.

SWSI Report Recommendation 20
(Please read this along with MWC recommendation 4)

Scottish Borders Council, together with its partners in NHS Borders and Lothian & Borders Police, should ensure multi-agency and multi-disciplinary co-ordination of complex cases at a sufficiently senior level to provide appropriate management oversight, effective information sharing and accountable practice. Arrangements should include a mechanism for the articulation and resolution of disputes between staff.

Evidence of progress implementing recommendation 20

Evidence of progress from record scrutiny

This is covered in detail under Mental Welfare Commission recommendation 4.

From document scrutiny

Scottish Borders Council and NHS Borders had a dispute resolution protocol. There was an (unsigned, undated) social work practice standards statement, which said recommendation 20 should be implemented. Scottish Borders Council had a (undated) Critical Information Exchange Protocol. This set out the arrangements for the co-ordinating of cases where there was joint involvement by social work and health.

From meetings and visits

There was an independently chaired multi-agency Adult Protection Committee. One of its roles was to oversee effective information sharing and accountable practice in complex protection of vulnerable adult cases.

There was a Critical Oversight Scrutiny Group which oversaw all protection of vulnerable adults matters. This group included the Chief Executive of Scottish Borders Council, the Chief Executive of NHS Borders and the Lothian and Borders Police Divisional Commander. The Police Divisional Commander (or a delegated senior officer) did a weekly review of all ongoing vulnerable adult investigations. David Hume the Chief Executive of Scottish Borders Council said:

> *"The future lies with those managers who can demonstrate the capacity to work effectively across organisational boundaries (Lord Laming in his Report on the Victoria Climbie Inquiry) This is the way forward for us as senior managers. Scottish Borders Council has a crystal clear commitment to the protection of vulnerable people".*

Chief Superintendent Common said;

> *"I am confident that this particular type of crime is, was, and will continue to be, investigated. We have not unearthed any new types of crime".*

We met with a group of Scottish Borders Council's elected members. Councillor Riddell-Carre said:

"A great change is taking place in our department. The current director holds monthly open forums with front line staff. It is important that front line staff have a say in how things could be done better. It is extremely important that record keeping is kept up to date and correct. There is more communication".

David Parker the leader of the council said:

"We have appointed a new director, Andrew Lowe, and have restructured staff. There has been a great amount of staff training. The key issues are embedding good practice and additional funds to recruit staff. We have been working through the action plan, reviewing work done and embedding good practice".

From staff interviews

Most of the staff interviewed said there was much greater commitment to the protection of vulnerable adults with learning disabilities. Most spoke about enhanced commitment at senior management level and downward in Scottish Borders Council and NHS Borders. One social worker said:

"Communication was a problem in the past. Managers would be told things and the issue would go into a black hole. Things are much improved. There is now very good leadership, particularly at team level. I feel valued and supported".

Another social worker said:

"There has been a lot of restructuring of the social work department. Now there is better access to managers. The profile of protection of vulnerable adults is now much higher".

On the disputes resolution protocol, a nurse said when they dealt with a dispute:

"Tried to sort it out first. Involved client then line manager. Never needed the Dispute Resolution Protocol".

A social worker said when they had an issue with a colleague:

"Tried to resolve it locally and using the line management system. Aware of protocol to resolve disputes but never used it".

Evidence of work still to be done

From meetings and visits

Education was not yet represented on the Adult Protection Committee.

From staff interviews

One group of staff said:

> *"There are some difficulties in getting all agencies to agree on risk assessments for individuals".*

Conclusion

We found some good progress implementing this recommendation. However, Education needed to be represented on the Adult Protection Committee. The vulnerable adults protection unit needed to be fully operational as a matter of urgency.

SWSI Report Recommendation 21

> The Department of Lifelong Care should ensure that when a referral concerning the well-being of an vulnerable adult is received from a professional, the fact of that referral is confirmed in writing by the referrer within 48 hours, and a written acknowledgement issued to the referrer by social work staff.

Evidence of progress implementing recommendation 21

Evidence of progress from record scrutiny

Protection of vulnerable adult with learning disabilities social work cases where there is specific harm or neglect allegation (n = 8)
In 1 out of 2 cases, social work staff issued a written acknowledgement of the referral within 48 hours. (N/A – 6)

There was insufficient data in the eight relevant cases to confirm if social workers were writing consistently to referrers within 48 hours.

Evidence of work still to be done

From document scrutiny

There was no reference in the social work procedures (Social Work Community Care Manual) to notifying referrers within 48 hours. There was guidance on responding to reports from members of the *public*:

> *"Where a report is received from a member of the public, the member of staff receiving the referral should reassure them that their report will be investigated".*

In addition, there was guidance on how other professionals should be informed about investigation *after* the investigation:

> *"All reports received from other professional agencies should be acknowledged and the investigating social worker should inform the agency in writing of the outcome of the initial investigation within seven days of its completion". (social work community care manual).*

Conclusion

Professionals making a referral should be written to within 48 hours. This timescale should be stated clearly in multi-agency vulnerable adult procedures. Compliance should be monitored by line managers and the new vulnerable adults protection unit. The reporting procedure is to be included within the social work management information system, but this was not done at the time of the inspection.

SWSI Report Recommendation 22

> **The Department of Lifelong Care should ensure that when a professional from another agency expresses concern to the department about its handling of a case, a senior manager reviews the file, meets and speaks to the professional concerned, and records in the case file the outcome of the discussion.**

Evidence of progress implementing recommendation 22

Evidence of progress from record scrutiny

None of the protection of vulnerable adults case records scrutinised had a specific example of a professional from another agency expressing concern about the handling of a case. Thus, it is not possible to verify implementation of recommendation 22 from the extensive record scrutiny exercise.

From document scrutiny

There was a clear joint disputes resolution protocol in place. There was a practice standards statement (undated, unsigned) that stated that recommendation 22 should be implemented.

From interviews with staff

The majority of the staff we interviewed were well aware of the dispute resolution protocol. They said they would be prepared to use this if required although none had done so to date (see previous staff quotes).

From visits and meetings

The dispute resolution protocol was referred to at a number of meetings. We found no information from any sources about this procedure being used.

Evidence of work still to be done

From record scrutiny

As stated, it was not possible to verify implementation of recommendation 22 from the case record scrutiny exercise.

From document scrutiny

We could not tell how the use of the disputes resolution protocol was monitored.

Conclusion

We found policies and procedures had been implemented to meet this recommendation. However, senior managers required to scrutinise more case records to check this recommendation was being implemented effectively. We were impressed by staff's awareness of dispute resolution.

SWSI Report Recommendation 23

> **The Department of Lifelong Care should develop a system of regular peer/management review of practice to encourage the positive identification of difficulties within a learning environment, and so promote continuous improvement.**

Evidence of progress implementing recommendation 23

Evidence of progress from record scrutiny

Scrutiny of social work supervision notes
There was evidence that supervision had been carried out regularly and the quantity and quality had improved significantly in the last 18 months.

From scrutiny of documents

A new social work department supervision and appraisal policy was provided. We found evidence it was being implemented.

A professional practice advisor had been appointment to audit and provide feedback on professional practice. Some audits were provided which indicated significant improvements in professional practice.

The social work department had introduced locality managers forums, peer practice groups and quality circles. The aim was to improve the quality of social work services.

An NHS Borders critical incident review process had been developed to review practice and identify shared learning.

There was a Whistle-blowing Policy which ensured that staff could report dangerous or poor practice. One day services worker said:

> *"I would use the whistle-blowing procedures. The alternative is to report to the line manager to make concerns known and seek action. I have challenged colleagues about behaviour/actions in the past, but not that often".*

An NHS staff member said:

> *"The Whistle-blowing Policy is a significant improvement".*

A social worker said:

> *"I would report any colleague who was not doing their job properly and putting any service user at risk".*

The Scottish Consortium for Learning Disability (SCLD) training programme included a new course entitled "Team Works". This was aimed at encouraging staff to acknowledge mistakes, learn from them and challenge others in the team in a constructive manner.

The training programme submitted included supervision skills for managers to ensure that managers had the skills and knowledge to provide supervision to staff to meet the required standards.

From meetings and visits

A specialist social work learning disability team had been established. There were plans for a joint social work and NHS learning disability team to be co-located. Premises had been identified. Senior staff said they spent more time with front line staff. Senior staff said this had been beneficial.

From interviews with staff, people with learning disabilities and family carers

Staff said supervision and training had increased and improved. Supervision was used to establish thresholds and clarify expectations, issues and roles.

Team leaders met for support and to ensure consistency applying the Protection of Vulnerable Adults Procedures.

Evidence of work still to be done

From the record scrutiny

All social work cases (n = 61)
In 77% of case records there was no sign of input from supervision sessions.

From scrutiny of documents

We found little evidence that action points identified in previous supervision sessions had been implemented. Supervision notes were not always signed by the supervisor.

Personal development plans or progress was not always indicated in supervision notes. We found little evidence of oversight by senior managers.

From meetings and visits

The vulnerable adults protection unit had not yet been established. This would have helped with implementation of the monitoring and supervision policies.

Conclusion

We found significant improvement in peer/management review of practice. Staff mentioned increased support through supervision and training.

Mental Welfare Commission Recommendation 1

> The role and function of the Borders Learning Disability Service should be reviewed to ensure that the service addresses the health needs of persons with a learning disability and children. Special attention should be paid to communication and to the clarity of roles and responsibilities within the Team. We support the proposal in the Borders Strategy for Adults with a Learning Disability that there should be a single community learning disability service formed from NHS Borders and social work learning disability services with a single manager. Our recommendations would apply equally to a joint service.

Evidence of progress implementing recommendation 1

Evidence of progress from record scrutiny

All social work records (n=61)	
Is the person with learning disabilities getting a service commensurate with *"The same as you?"*	Yes - 77% No – 21% N/A – 1%
How effectively is *"The same as you"* impacting on this person?	High impact – 20% Some impact – 49% Low impact – 31%

Health records community learning disability team (n=8)

We found the state of the files varied. Some were well detailed, with a good record of visits, others had correspondence only. Risk assessments were included in 5 of the 8 files. We found evidence of joint working in all of the files, with information sent to all relevant parties. A record of all staff involved was in half of the files. We found evidence of information being shared on a routine basis. Where there was a concern of abuse, we found evidence of good communication between agencies. There was a risk assessment and care plan in 3 of the 4 files.

The psychiatrist had discharged some cases in which there had been no contact for sometime. We could not tell what involvement the community learning disability team would have, if any, in these cases. However, the GP could refer again to the community learning disability team at any time if necessary. There was one very poor health care assessment. There was also one excellent file which had very good information about the involvement with the person with learning disabilities and relevant others.

From document scrutiny

There was a fully comprehensive Joint Learning Disability Strategy for adults. This had a service plan for the integration of NHS Borders and Scottish Borders Council learning disability services. This was fully costed and was intended to be in place by October 2005. We saw a Strategy for Health Services for Children with Learning Disabilities. A project manager for managing the process of integrating health and social work learning disability services was appointed in April 2004. There were planning papers on the integration of the services. We found evidence staff feel some ownership of the strategy.

The NHS community learning disability team had produced a leaflet with information for people who wish to refer someone to the learning disability service. The role and function of the Borders community learning disability team was clear. More could be done to distribute the leaflet to places where it would be read.

From meetings and visits

The Mental Health and Learning Disabilities Network had taken a thorough approach to planning and implementing clinical governance. There had been some efforts to find out the health needs of people with learning disabilities in the Borders.

There was a new learning disability social work team, managed by a social work manager. NHS Borders first appointed a service manager for learning disability in November 2004. This post is currently vacant.

There were key appointments, to manage the joint service and NHS Borders community learning disability team. This would provide a joint social work/health manager and clinical leadership to the community learning disability team. A fully integrated community learning disability team was planned for October 2005.

We heard from staff and people with learning disabilities about some difficulties in accessing community learning disability team services:

- Waiting time for referral to the community learning disability team could be up to 9 weeks;

- The community learning disability team had vacancies for psychology and for occupational therapy, causing delays in referral and access to some specialist services;

- We had some concerns about the skill mix of the community learning disability team and the community learning disability resource; and

- There was no consultant psychiatrist cover for children with learning disabilities and mental health problems.

Evidence of work still to be done

- There is a need to evaluate how the protection of vulnerable adults training has impacted on day to day practice.

- NHS Borders has failed to recruit to its vacant learning disability service manager post. It has put in place a temporary arrangement with a senior nurse, senior allied health professional and consultant psychiatrist working as a management team. There is a need to recruit a single joint community learning disability team manager quickly.

- There was a lack of capacity within teams to work with victims and perpetrators, and the lack of psychology input was a major gap in services.

- Care management arrangement – a number of nursing staff were reluctant to become care managers as they feared this would mean lack of opportunity to maintain their nursing skills.

- Links to GP practices – not all practices were aware of role of the (NHS) team or could name the relevant link nurse.

- Details of the formalised joint budgets and funding of integrated team to be agreed.

- Protocol for sharing information exists for Scottish Borders Council team, but not for NHS team. A joint protocol exists (dated 21/02/02) but little evidence that this is a detailed enough for use or operational.

- Caseload management – more clarity is needed on how members of the NHS team divide their time.

- There is no service for young people and children with learning disabilities who have severe challenging behaviour and mental health problems. This group is vulnerable, both as potential victims and perpetrators of abuse. NHS Borders needs to act on its strategy and develop a service for children.

- Some people with learning disabilities who are in the Hume Unit (NHS in-patient services) had their discharge delayed. The Hume Unit is an environment inappropriate to the needs of the people living there.

- Continuity of care for out of area placements (current and future).

Conclusion

On the protection of vulnerable adults with learning disabilities, we found convincing evidence to show well-planned strategic development of the service. The delegation of clinical responsibilities in the service is clear. A single team approach has been adopted. At practitioner level staff were still adjusting to the changes in their role and function in a new integrated service. Regular evaluation of the service at all levels is needed to ensure that the new service will deliver agreed outcomes for people with learning disabilities. There is a key role for clinical governance, staff appraisal and training.

Mental Welfare Commission Recommendation 2

NHS Borders should provide guidance for staff on roles, responsibilities and communication within primary care services, acute services and learning disability services in cases involving people with a learning disability where there is multi-disciplinary involvement.

Evidence of progress implementing recommendation 2

Evidence of progress from record scrutiny

Issue	All social work records (n=61)	Vulnerable adult cases (n=20)	Health records (n=37)	Transition cases (n=8)
Are there clear contact details for key agencies and key staff?	Yes 85%			
Is there evidence of effective multi-agency joint working?	Yes 84%			
Is there evidence of good interagency communication about protection issues?		Yes 95%		
Is there evidence of joint work to protect the person with learning disabilities?		Yes 95%		
Even if they didn't attend, has the service passed copies of minutes (of case conferences) to all relevant bodies?		Yes 85%		
Are all of the relevant transition planning partners involved? (in transition planning).				Yes 7
Is there evidence of joint working and sharing information?			Yes 80%	
Is there a record of all professionals involved?			Yes 48%	

Evidence from scrutiny of documents,

There was a joint social work department, NHS Borders protocol/eligibility criteria for when a person with learning disabilities received the Care Programme Approach.

There was some training about the Adults with Incapacity Act (Part 5) and consent to treatment policies for staff in learning disability and primary care and acute care. This training had not yet been audited. Training about the new Mental Health Act for staff across the services was at an early stage.

We liked a primary and community services toolkit for vulnerable adults (April 2005). However, we could not tell how its use would be evaluated.

There was written guidance, with related protocols, to clarify the roles and responsibilities and communication within primary care services, acute services and learning disability services. Scrutiny of records suggested that communication about protection issues between different parts of the service was generally good.

A review of the number of professional development plans in place was conducted in 2004. An independent audit of professional development plans was in progress. We heard of plans to "map" training needs analysis and professional development plans onto the new Joint Learning Disability Strategy. This was a laudable aim, but seemed to be a long way off, given the number of staff still awaiting professional development plans and regular staff appraisal. Neither appraisal training nor staff appraisal across the service appeared to be done consistently or systematically. The audit done in 2004 needs repeated to check improvements.

From meetings and visits

Staff based at the Borders General Hospital worked closely with the learning disability service and other providers to plan comprehensive care for people who had a learning disability and complex needs.

The Chair of the new Primary and Community Services Board made sure the needs of people with a learning disability were met by primary care. We were impressed with the professional commitment and enthusiasm for this work.

In 2004, the Local Health Care Co-operative (LHCC) looked at information about people with learning disabilities in GP practices. More than 50% had variable levels of databases. A single database template was offered to all GP practices.

Single shared assessment would be used to share information about adults with learning disabilities. This had been piloted at the time of the joint inspection and was being slowly introduced across the service (less than 20 people at the time of the joint inspection). A risk assessment was incorporated into the single shared assessment. The documentation had symbols and was clearly laid out. We found some adults with learning disabilities had person centred plans. Learning disability nursing staff did the initial holistic health assessment. Other disciplines contributed where necessary.

One example of multi-disciplinary involvement was the social work emergency duty team, covering all of the Borders. They reported frequent contact with health professionals at Borders General Hospital, duty GPs and learning disability services. The emergency duty team kept lists of adults with learning disabilities, vulnerable adults (including people with learning disabilities), appropriate adults and people subject to Guardianship orders. There was some sharing of this information with social work colleagues, but limited sharing with health staff. A major issue raised by staff was the lack of clarity over cases in which vulnerability issues over-ride consent issues and information is to be shared.

Interviews with staff

One social work manager said:

"There is more direction and focus for activity. Personnel and personalities have changed and there is a greater sense of working together".

An NHS manager said:

"The learning disabilities team has access to a range of practitioners who can assist social work, health professionals such as occupational therapists, physiotherapists, speech therapists, music therapists and psychologists".

A social worker said:

"There is much more awareness of interagency working now".

Another social worker said:

"Joint working with health colleagues, district nurses and GPs in case conferences has been good".

A social work team leader said:

"Huge commitment to make the learning disability service a good one at all levels and real commitment to the integration programme".

Evidence of work still to be done

We found no specialist services in allied health professions for children with learning disabilities, but they were seen on an equitable and accessible basis by the paediatric services. Children and young people who had learning disabilities and mental health problems had no specialist psychiatry. The Learning Disability Transitions to Adult Services Joint Working Group produced a report which highlighted the need for continuity of care across all services.

Conclusion

We found NHS Borders provided clear guidance on roles and responsibilities. We found staff understood the guidance. Communication appeared generally good despite some gaps. New initiatives will improve the situation further. NHS Borders should evaluate the impact of their actions, particularly in relation to how primary and acute care see the role of the learning disability services.

Mental Welfare Commission Recommendation 3

General practitioners and primary health care services in the Borders should be made aware of and have easy access to information about the needs of people who have a learning disability. Services must be flexible and delivered in a way that recognises and accommodates any special requirements of persons with a learning disability. Appropriate liaison and support from the specialist learning disability services should be in place in line with Promoting Health Supporting Inclusion, NHS QIS Learning Disability Quality Indicators and NHS Health Scotland Learning Disability Needs Assessment Report.

Evidence of progress implementing recommendation 3

Evidence of progress from record scrutiny

Not applicable.

From scrutiny of documents

There was an NHS Borders draft "Health Improvement Strategy for People with Learning Disabilities". This did not have specific objectives, a timescale or costings.

From meetings and visits

There was an NHS Borders steering group responsible for implementing the recommendations in 'Promoting Health Supporting Inclusion'. There was a conference for nurses in April 2004 to communicate proposed changes. These included new initiatives in nurse education, health promotion, transitions from child to adult services, specialist service provision and specialist liaison posts in hospitals. Training materials were intended to provide GPs and primary care staff with educational sessions and self-paced training materials.

In the two GP practices we saw, there was evidence of variability in relation to learning disability awareness and links to the community learning disability team. One health centre we visited was an example of good practice. Staff were well-informed. There was a community learning disability nurse linked to the practice. Record keeping was excellent. There was good communication within the primary care team and with other professionals and other parts of primary care. By contrast, staff at another health centre were not aware of any community learning disability nurses linked to the practice. There was poor awareness of learning disability issues and a negative attitude to dealing with the learning disability services.

The failure, at GP practice level, to identify and pass on relevant information relating to vulnerable adults was a key finding of the Mental Welfare Commission's Report. As recently as May 2005 the Chief Medical Officer for Scotland wrote to all GPs emphasising the responsibilities of GPs dealing with people with learning disabilities.

GPs had been offered vulnerable adult protection training, but at the time of the inspection, no GPs had taken up this training. This was disappointing. A separate training event for GPs was planned for 26 October 2005, as part of the Time for Multi-

Disciplinary Education (TiME) programme. More than half the primary health care teams have had training, delivered on-site.

Learning disability services were accessed via GPs, service referral or self-referrals. Each practice had a "link" community nurse from the learning disability team. One of three nurses was the named link for each GP practice in the Borders. Although the three nurses had a list of their allocated practices, not all GP practices were able to name their link nurse, or give information on their roles and responsibilities.

Adults and young people with learning disabilities attended well woman/well man clinics. Attendance was not monitored specifically for people with learning disabilities. There were tentative plans for a public health nurse for minority and socially excluded groups.

A learning disability liaison nurse had been appointed. Her impact, in liaising with and informing primary care staff, was most noticeable at the Borders General Hospital. We found her impact was less evident elsewhere in community services and in specialist services.

No specific arrangements were in place to identify and support the communication needs of children and adults with learning disabilities admitted to hospital. For example, learning disability speech and language therapists and acute speech and language therapists were not routinely told when people with learning disabilities were admitted.

The training and development department records attendance of primary care staff at training events related to the needs of children and adults with learning disabilities. Staff interviewed liked the "investigation to case conference" training.

There was a plan to have a list of good practice "champions" for Promoting Health Supporting Inclusion across the Borders.

NHS Borders had modified their existing complaints procedure. There was an easy read leaflet, "*I Want to Complain*".

NHS Borders and Scottish Borders Council commissioned a range of advocacy services. Funding to support advocacy (2004-2007) was inadequate to meet all priority needs. The advocacy plan for 2004-2007 mentioned children with learning disabilities.

The chart on next page shows what people with learning disabilities said about advocacy.

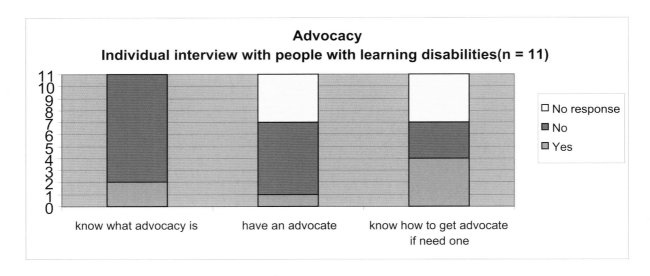

Interviews with people with learning disabilities

The chart below shows what people with learning disabilities said about health issues.

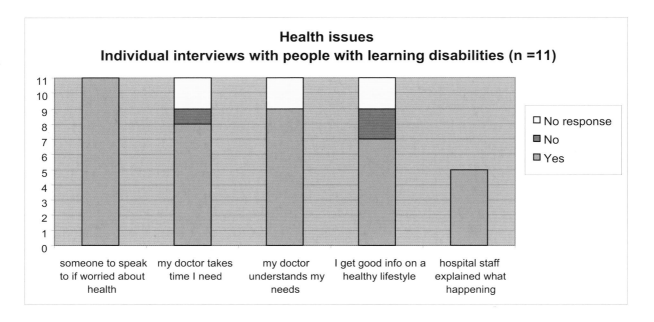

People with learning disabilities said:

> "My GP is very good".

> "I would go to all the GPs, they are all nice".

Conclusion

NHS Borders had tried hard to make information about the special needs of people with learning disabilities available to GPs and primary care staff. The chair of the new Primary and Community Services Board had raised the profile of the needs of people with learning disabilities in primary care. The community learning disability services and the liaison nurse should make sure that all GP practices know about how the learning disability team operates and what it can offer. Uptake of vulnerable adult training by GPs needs to be carefully monitored. Primary care services need to be more aware of the role of the liaison nurse.

Mental Welfare Commission Recommendation 4

NHS Borders, along with its partners in Scottish Borders Council and Borders Police, should ensure multi-disciplinary co-ordination of complex cases involving people with learning disability where more than one agency is involved. The co-ordination should be at a sufficiently senior level to provide appropriate management oversight, effective information sharing and accountable practice. Arrangements should include a mechanism for the resolution of case management disputes between staff.

Evidence of progress implementing recommendation 4

Evidence of progress from record scrutiny

Health records: relating to 12 adults, 10 subject to Welfare Guardianship (n = 37)	Social Work records for adults with complex disabilities and high support needs (n = 10)	All social work cases (n = 61)
48% of the files had clear contact details for key agencies and key staff involved.	90% of records had clear contact details for key agencies and key staff involved. 10% did not.	85% had clear contact details for key agencies and key staff.
There was evidence of effective multi-agency joint working in 80% of the files.	There was evidence of effective multi-agency joint working in 70% of cases.	There was evidence of effective multi-agency joint working in 83% of the files.
72% had clear, prominent information that the person had a learning disability and 75% had a summary of the person's needs.	There was evidence that the first line manager regularly scrutinised 60% of the files.	Where there were concerns about abuse, in 95% of the files, there was evidence of good interagency communication and a clear protection plan in 85% of the records
Of the 8 cases where there were concerns of abuse, 5 files had up to date information and a clear care and protection plan.	Important events were highlighted in 90% of case files.	There was one Guardianship case however, where there was no allocated social worker for a year, and the health professional involved was unaware of the risks. This situation has now been addressed.

From scrutiny of documents

Scottish Borders Council and NHS Borders had an information sharing protocol. They also have operational guidelines for Care Programme Approach. All of the policy and procedure documents we examined said there were processes in place to ensure multi-disciplinary co-ordination of complex cases. The documents also referred to overview by managers.

From meetings and visits

All complex cases had been identified by the learning disability teams, and care managers identified. Regular reviews, chaired by managers, were taking place. The Care Programme Approach was used to manage the care for 12 individuals. The numbers were likely to increase once the single service was established.

We heard case presentations which demonstrated very thoughtful and reflective practice. There was a real sense of teamwork, an understanding of each others roles and skills, and good evidence of information sharing and management overview of these complex cases.

We found evidence of good links between the police, the social work out of hours service and the general hospital. We found effective links between the social work out of hours service and Border Care Alarms and Borderline.

From interviews with staff, people with learning disabilities and family carers

The district nurses all said they had good links with social workers and always attended case conferences and received minutes of the meetings. One nurse said:

> *"The biggest change is joint working and communication is much better now. There is far more face to face communication with social workers".*

Another nurse said:

> *"People are not so precious about their roles and there are clear lines of accountability".*

From the interviews with 11 people with learning disabilities, 10 had a social worker and all said that there was someone who took time to listen to them (either a social worker or someone else).

Evidence of work still to be done

From record scrutiny

All records should highlight that the person has a learning disability and have clear contact details of the key agencies and staff involved with them.
All health staff working with vulnerable people need to have a copy of the risk assessment and risk management plan and the key contact person.
The accident & emergency records have a tick box for unexplained injury if the person is a child or over 75. It would be helpful to include all vulnerable groups.

From scrutiny of documents

The Service Plan for Adults with Learning Disability is still a draft document.

The social work supervision template did not clearly set out protection issues for vulnerable adults with learning disabilities. This could easily be rectified and also be used by health staff.

Currently, there were no shared records nor links with database/records with NHS Borders and the Council.

From meetings and visits

Once the joint health and social work learning disability team is in place, further guidance will be required for managing complex cases under the single service.

We found no easily accessible joint database to monitor and review all out of area placements. There was no standardised multi-agency review process for out of area placements.

From interviews with staff, people with learning disabilities and family carers

Staff and family carers said there was very little contact between children and adult services. This was an area that required to be addressed. One NHS member of staff said:

> *"Consultant meets social worker and education at future needs stage, but at present don't talk to each other enough".*

Conclusion

We found staff were committed to providing a responsive service to people with complex needs and working jointly with others. Improved integrated records would help greatly.

Mental Welfare Commission Recommendation 5

> **The Implementation of the Vulnerable Adults Policy in the Borders should be monitored, reviewed and evaluated to ensure the needs of vulnerable persons with a learning disability are recognised and responded to by Health and Social Work Services and their partners in Lothian and Borders Police. This should take account of Recommendation 23 of the "The same as you?" report published in May 2000, which states, 'The appropriate agencies should develop policies and guidelines on protecting vulnerable adults. Social Work Departments should review their procedures on guardianship to include making a formal assessment of risk a normal part of deciding whether an application should be made.**

Evidence of progress implementing recommendation 5

Evidence of progress from record scrutiny

Health records where there were concerns about abuse (n = 8)	Social Work records protection of vulnerable adult with LD cases (n = 20)	All social work records (n = 61)
In 4 cases, important events were highlighted and files were up to date.	In 95% of cases, important events were highlighted and in 90% of cases, files were up to date.	In 72% of cases, important events were highlighted and in 82% of cases files were up to date.
In 5 cases, there was a risk assessment, care and protection plan.	In 95% of cases, there was a risk assessment, care and protection plan.	In 74% of cases there was a risk assessment.
There was evidence of effective joint working in 87% of the files.	There was evidence of effective joint working in 95% of files.	There was evidence of effective joint working in 84% of files.
There was evidence of good interagency communication about protection issues in 6 files.	In 95% of cases there was evidence of good interagency communication about protection issues.	N/A
5 files had case conference minutes.	The purpose of the reports was clearly indicated in 95% of cases.	The purpose of the reports was clearly indicated in 72% of cases.
Vulnerable Adults procedures were followed in 7 cases.	Vulnerable Adults procedures were followed in 95% of cases.	N/A

From scrutiny of documents

Joint interagency protection of vulnerable adult procedures were implemented in 2003. There was a mandatory educational programme for staff. Annual refresher training took place. The corporate induction programme made staff aware of the protection of vulnerable adult procedures. We found the training materials were of good quality and protocols easy to follow.

An audit of health and social work staff awareness of the procedures had been done. This highlighted some gaps in knowledge as well as numbers of staff still requiring training.

Risk assessments were undertaken as part of single shared assessments, welfare Guardianship policies and procedures had been developed.

From meetings and visits

Training had also been undertaken by the independent sector and advocacy services. We found there was good awareness of the protection of vulnerable adults from all of independent sector representatives we met.

Staff told us that the vulnerable adults procedures were on the intranet. They also had easy access to paper copies.

We found staff at the accident and emergency and the admission wards at Borders General Hospital knew about the protection of vulnerable adults procedures.

The Vulnerable Adult Protection Committee had good representation from a variety of relevant agencies. The criminal justice system was represented by the police, Procurator Fiscal Service and Reporter to the Children's Panel.

From interviews with staff, people with learning disabilities and family carers

Staff from the independent sector said that information about the protection of vulnerable adults was not reaching front line staff. However, all front line staff we interviewed from NHS Borders and Scottish Borders Council, were well trained and knowledgeable about the protection of vulnerable adults.

The new mental health team leader provided support and guidance to all mental health officers operating throughout the council. Her previous experience working with Adults with Incapacity legislation was valuable when considering whether Welfare Guardianship was required.

A district nurse who had used the procedures recently found them easy to follow and that all agencies involved had worked well together.

Most staff found the Investigation to Case Conference course stimulating and useful for joint working and networking.

The people with learning disabilities we interviewed all said they felt safe. They knew who to talk to if they were worried or frightened.

Evidence of work still to be done

From record scrutiny

Health records where there were concerns about abuse (n = 8)
Only 5 health records had a risk assessment and care and protection plan (n = 8).
Communication can always be improved.
Case conference minutes were only present in 5 of the health records (n = 8).

From scrutiny of documents

The recommendations from the audit of staff awareness of the guidelines was being actioned.

The vulnerable adults training should be evaluated.

From meetings and visits

Some procedures needed further development including standardisation of the reporting format.

The vulnerable adult protection unit as a new establishment, required operational guidelines and a system to evaluate its effectiveness.

People with learning disabilities should be on the Adult Protection Committee.

An additional course is being offered for GPs in October 2005. The learning outcomes will be evaluated and refresher training should also be made available to GPs.

Conclusion

We found co-operation between agencies had improved. Further inclusion of people with learning disabilities was required. Staff and managers stated that the training had been effective and that they were clear what was expected of them to safeguard and protect vulnerable people. Again, better shared information would be valuable.

Mental Welfare Commission Recommendation 6

> **The discharge policy and procedures of Borders General Hospital should give guidance on the needs of patients who have a learning disability. Liaison arrangements between learning disability services and acute hospital services in the Borders should be in line with "Promoting Health Supporting Inclusion" and the recent NHS Health Scotland Learning Disability Health Needs Assessment Report and NHS QIS revised Learning Disability Quality Indicators (both published on 23 February 2004)**

Evidence of progress implementing recommendation 6

Evidence of progress from record scrutiny

The health records we scrutinised at Borders General Hospital were up to date. We found some evidence of joint working between primary/acute/learning disability services.

From scrutiny of documents

The discharge policy covered all vulnerable adults, including people with learning disabilities. Staff had received specific guidance about people with learning disabilities. The care pathways were clear and responsibilities of different staff were clearly stated.

From meetings and visits

The staff in all areas of Borders General Hospital showed genuine and well informed concern for the welfare of patients with learning disabilities. Patients with learning disabilities were prioritised in accident and emergency. Staff had a good understanding of consent and adults with incapacity issues.

A primary care/acute learning disability liaison nurse was now in post. We met with her and heard how she had been working with medical staff at Borders General Hospital to raise awareness about people with learning disabilities. She worked with staff in the hospital on the objectives set in "Promoting Health Supporting Inclusion". Four people had been referred to her over three months.

Interviews with people with learning disabilities

All five of the people with learning disabilities interviewed individually who had been in hospital recently, said that doctors and nurses explained what was happening to them.

All eleven of the people with learning disabilities interviewed individually said there was someone they could speak to if they were worried about their health.

Only one out of eleven people with learning disabilities interviewed individually, said their doctor did not take the time with them that they needed.

Seven out of eleven people with learning disabilities interviewed individually, said they had had information about leading a healthy life.

One person with learning disabilities who had spent time in hospital said:

"They were marvellous, exceptional. Lots of detail".

Another said about their doctor spending enough time:

"She certainly does and drew pictures of what my operation would be".

Interviews with family carers

One of the family carers interviewed individually said they were not involved in discharge planning/procedures when the person they cared for was discharged from hospital.

One family carer said of a period when the person they care for was unwell:

"A learning disability team was brought in. He had a psychiatrist, a psychologist, a psychiatric nurse, a nurse, a GP, and a social worker all at the same time".

Evidence of work still to be done

From record scrutiny

Information was routinely sent to GPs, but not copied to the community learning disability team. The records did not clearly state which other professionals were involved. We found the accident and emergency record had tick boxes for unexplained injury if the person was a child or over 75. It would be helpful to include *all* vulnerable groups.

Conclusion

We found communication between Borders General Hospital and learning disability services had improved considerably in the past year. The discharge policy took the needs of people with learning disabilities into account. Staff found it easy to understand and use. The liaison nurse was improving practice in line with "Promoting Health Supporting Inclusion. NHS Borders should evaluate the effectiveness of this post.

Mental Welfare Commission Recommendation 7

NHS Borders and Scottish Borders Council should ensure that all appropriate staff are aware of the importance of informal carers and their rights to a carer's assessment.

Evidence of progress implementing recommendation 7

Evidence of progress from record scrutiny

Health records (25 scrutinised)	Social Work records: adults with complex disabilities and high support needs living at home. (2 scrutinised)	All social work records (29 scrutinised family carer present)
No assessments appeared to have been offered nor was there any apparent understanding of the purpose.	1 carer had an up to date carers assessment.	In 28% of relevant cases, there was an up to date carers assessment.

From scrutiny of documents

The carers assessment form written by the Princess Royal Trust for Carers, NHS Borders and Scottish Borders Council, was comprehensive. Carers can self assess or be assisted to complete the form with the help of any professional using the guidance provided.

From meetings and visits

We were informed that the forms were relatively new and in the early stages of implementation. We could not tell what assessment tool was in place before.

One of the case studies in the vulnerable adult protection training course involved a carer. Staff who had done that training did not know about carers' assessments.

From interviews with staff, people with learning disabilities and family carers

All four family carers we interviewed individually and two family carers we interviewed as a group did not know about carers' assessments. They were not sure if they had had one done. One carer (group interview) had a carer's assessment the previous week. One carer said:

> *"I would have liked the assessment when I was taking care of my son and shown different ways of doing things. No one listened to me or was interested".*

Another said of carers assessments:

> *"I would definitely want one".*

The nurses said that all carers were offered an assessment when they were carrying out a single shared assessment of the cared-for person, but no one had ever asked for one. They had not seen the forms and assumed that social workers completed the assessments.

One social worker said:

> *"Carers assessments are low priority, unless there is conflict."*

One social worker said:

> *"Felt embarrassed about lack of knowledge (of carers assessments) but now more confident. Feel this is well supported through policy".*

A social worker in the children affected by disability team said:

> *"I am now doing one or two carers assessments a month".*

Another social worker said:

> *"I have done one carers assessment. Carers needs are taken into account in the assessment of the cared-for person".*

Very few staff knew about carers' rights to be offered an assessment, but they stated that they were aware of the needs of carers.

Evidence of work still to be done

From the record scrutiny

Scottish Borders Council and NHS Borders should develop a performance appraisal tool to monitor the numbers and the quality of carer assessments.

From scrutiny of documents

Carers must be given information about their rights and the assessment process. Carers' policy, procedures and practice guidelines could be reinforced through staff briefing sessions.

From meetings and visits

Carers need to be treated more as partners in the assessment and care planning process. Carers issues should be a standing item in staff supervision sessions.

All practitioners needed to acknowledge the importance of carers.

Joint agency training needed to give information on the carers' legislation, policy and practice guidelines, the carer relationship and the framework tool for carer assessments. Carers should be involved in delivering the training.

Conclusion

We found some evidence of more attention being given to carers' assessment. Lack of information on the benefits of a carers' assessment may be a hindrance.

Mental Welfare Commission Recommendation 8

NHS Borders and Scottish Borders Council Social Work Services should carry out a review of record keeping for cases where there is multi-agency involvement.

Evidence of progress implementing recommendation 8

Evidence of progress from record scrutiny

Health records: 12 adults multiple files scrutinised (n = 37)	Social Work records for the same 12 adults
76% of files were up to date	92%
There is evidence of continuous recording in 55% of cases	92%
In 80% of cases entries were clear, signed and dated	92%
In 75% of cases there was a summary of the person's needs	92%
There was evidence of joint working in 80% of cases	92%
There was evidence of regular reviews in 50% of cases	92%
There was evidence of sharing information in 80% of cases	92%
There was evidence of sharing care plans in 40% of cases	83%

From scrutiny of documents

We found a multi-agency audit had been carried out and joint actions agreed.

A completion of health records policy was distributed in April 2005 and due for review in April 2006. Social Work Community Care Recording Guidelines were issued in 2004. Managers from both health and social work had explicit responsibility for discussing and monitoring work through recording and signing to say they have done so.

Social work records were subject to systematic review by line managers through the supervision process. The responsibilities of health clinicians and managers were also clearly laid out, which included supervising compliance and addressing any issues through performance appraisal and personal development plans.

From meetings and visits

Work was in progress with both the integration of health records and joint health/ social work records.

From interviews with staff, people with learning disabilities and family carers

Although some staff felt that there was now a plethora of action plans, policies and procedures, they were all very clear about the importance of up to date case recording to justify decision making.

Staff have been issued with reminders of their responsibilities in relation to record keeping.

Evidence of work still to be done

From record scrutiny

54% of these social work records had been regularly scrutinised by a line manager.
No evidence of health managers inspecting files, but the policy had just been implemented prior to our visit.
The audit has highlighted areas for improvement, and joint actions have been agreed.

From meetings and visits

Work was underway to develop integrated records for the NHS community learning disability team. This needed to be monitored to check that timescales did not slip.

One GP practice had piloted a front sheet on case notes, which highlighted when a person has learning disability and/or is vulnerable. It was intended to roll this out across all GP practices. The information would be prominently displayed and easily accessible for locum or out of hours staff.

From interviews with staff, people with learning disabilities and family carers

The new systems were at the early stages of being integrated into supervision policy and practice. Senior managers required to act to make sure the case notes for complex cases with a learning disability, including GP notes, received regular audit.

Conclusion

We found good progress on improved record keeping and information sharing. Quality assurance systems had been implemented. NHS Borders need to ensure that NHS records continue to improve.

Mental Welfare Commission Recommendation 9

A dedicated dietetic service should form an integral part of Borders Learning disability services.

Evidence of progress implementing recommendation 9

Evidence of progress from health record scrutiny

Information from the dietician was appropriately shared with others. There was a good distribution of copy letters. However, the dietician was not copied into risk assessments.

From document scrutiny

A specialist dietician was appointed in November 2004. She worked half time (0.5) with the NHS community learning disability team. She provided well organised input to the learning disability services. She worked with both social work and primary care staff. She took referrals and worked directly with people with learning disabilities. She also acted in a support and advisory role.

Evidence of work still to be done

The dietician had yet to undergo protection of vulnerable adults training.

The Draft Child Health Strategy was not a joint document although it does mention partner agencies. The weakness in this approach was acknowledged by NHS Borders who saw this document as a pragmatic response to a clear and pressing service deficit in health. The draft document did not include dietetic input within phase one (for which funding is secured). Funding needs to be identified for specialist dietetic input.

Conclusion

We found the appointment of a 0.5 specialist dietician in November 2004 had improved the learning disability service. The dietician provided enthusiastic and professional input, and linked well to other professionals. Unless money is found, children with learning disabilities will not get a specialised dietician service.

Mental Welfare Commission Recommendation 10

> **NHS Borders should review existing policy and provide clear procedures to community nursing staff on the transfer of information between primary health care teams when patients move.**

Evidence of progress implementing recommendation 10

Evidence of progress from record scrutiny

Not applicable.

From scrutiny of documents

We found NHS Borders had clear procedures. The NHS transfer form provided detailed information which included areas of risk.

Discussions were held between the two district nurse teams when patients transferred to another area.

From meetings and visits

We found all practices used the forms and a flowchart had also been developed.

From interviews with staff, people with learning disabilities and family carers

All district nurses interviewed were aware of the transfer procedure and used it effectively.

Evidence of work still to be done

From meetings and visits

The form could be used by all health and local authority staff to transfer information at transition stages and for out of area placements.

Conclusion

We found NHS Borders had put systems in place to make sure information was transferred between primary health care teams when patients move.

Timeline

Would the abuse happen again?

When we went back to look at the services in the Borders, we wanted to know what Scottish Borders Council and NHS Borders had done to make their services better. We particularly wanted to know what might be different if the same situation where people were at risk of abuse and neglect, happened again. Would services respond better? Would there be less chance that people would be severely abused and neglected?

We looked at some of the events that happened leading up to the abuse of the vulnerable adults with learning disabilities who live in the Borders. Our previous reports showed that there were times when services could and should have acted but failed to do so. We made an assessment of how well they might respond if the same problems came to their attention now.

It is not possible to say that abuse can never happen. However, we think that people in the Scottish Borders can be assured that people providing services have learned from what happened. We have shown this by displaying some of the times when the services failed to act. We have shown what the various agencies have done about this. We think there is still more that they could do, but we think that the actions they have taken would make it much less likely that they would fail to safeguard vulnerable people in the same way again.

Follow-up to Borders Inquiries Timeline

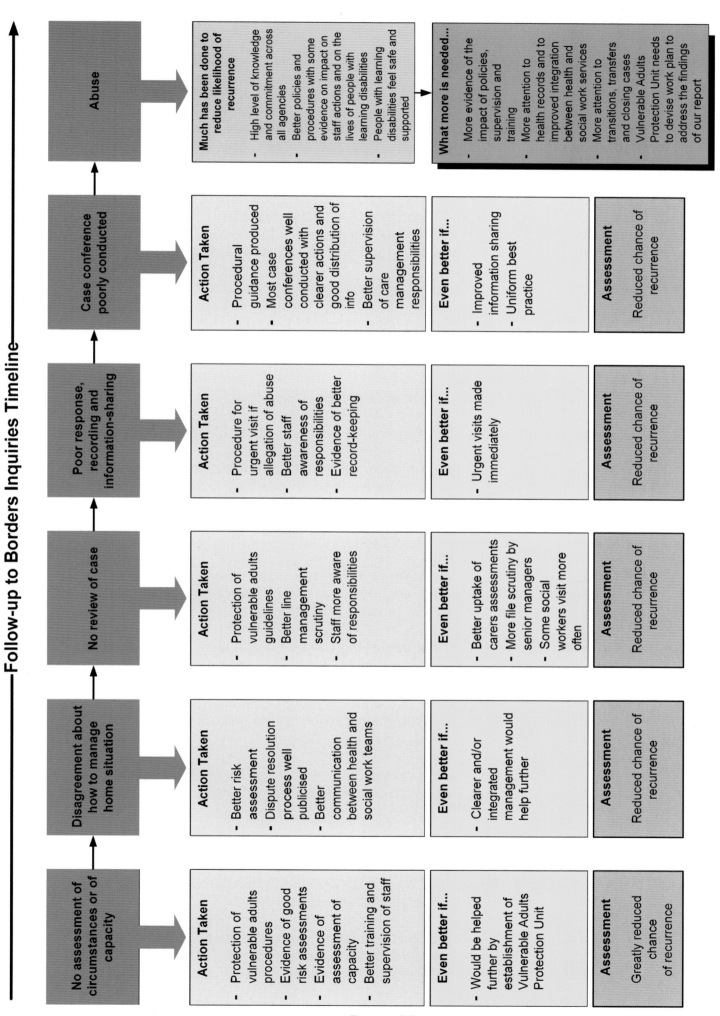

No assessment of circumstances or of capacity

Action Taken
- Protection of vulnerable adults procedures
- Evidence of good risk assessments
- Evidence of assessment of capacity
- Better training and supervision of staff

Even better if...
- Would be helped further by establishment of Vulnerable Adults Protection Unit

Assessment
Greatly reduced chance of recurrence

Disagreement about how to manage home situation

Action Taken
- Better risk assessment
- Dispute resolution process well publicised
- Better communication between health and social work teams

Even better if...
- Clearer and/or integrated management would help further

Assessment
Reduced chance of recurrence

No review of case

Action Taken
- Protection of vulnerable adults guidelines
- Better line management scrutiny
- Staff more aware of responsibilities

Even better if...
- Better uptake of carers assessments
- More file scrutiny by senior managers
- Some social workers visit more often

Assessment
Reduced chance of recurrence

Poor response, recording and information-sharing

Action Taken
- Procedure for urgent visit if allegation of abuse
- Better staff awareness of responsibilities
- Evidence of better record-keeping

Even better if...
- Urgent visits made immediately

Assessment
Reduced chance of recurrence

Case conference poorly conducted

Action Taken
- Procedural guidance produced
- Most case conferences well conducted with clearer actions and good distribution of info
- Better supervision of care management responsibilities

Even better if...
- Improved information sharing
- Uniform best practice

Assessment
Reduced chance of recurrence

Abuse

Much has been done to reduce likelihood of recurrence
- High level of knowledge and commitment across all agencies
- Better policies and procedures with some evidence on impact on staff actions and on the lives of people with learning disabilities
- People with learning disabilities feel safe and supported

What more is needed...
- More evidence of the impact of policies, supervision and training
- More attention to health records and to improved integration between health and social work services
- More attention to transitions, transfers and closing cases
- Vulnerable Adults Protection Unit needs to devise work plan to address the findings of our report

Good practice

Although this inspection was unique we hope the methodology used and the lessons learned will inform a more general joint inspection process. This will happen from 2005-2006 onwards.

To help with this, we have identified areas of good practice both in individual services and in joint working between and among services. The inspectors from all the agencies involved in the inspection have contributed to this section. We were impressed with the many examples of good practice we saw during the inspection.

We have listed the examples of good practice under four headings:

- Strategic level; leadership and management;

- Operational level; staff and staffing;

- Protection of vulnerable adults with learning disabilities; and

- Meeting practical needs and improving people's quality of life.

We hope these examples of good practice, will encourage others, across Scotland and beyond, to look at how they can improve the services they provide to people with learning disabilities and their families.

Strategic level; leadership and management

- **Co-operation**: The co-operation of all Borders council and Borders health colleagues and key stakeholders, including people with learning disabilities and family carers, in the inspection process.

- **Good leadership**: A fair number of the Borders social work staff interviewed said they felt there was good leadership from their senior managers.

- **Drive for improvement**: All of the staff interviewed said there had been an intense drive from the top to improve practice on the protection of vulnerable adults with learning disabilities.

- **Police information sharing protocol**: There is a protocol and ultimately a shared database may well be introduced. The relevant information does appear to be shared quickly.

- **Critical Oversight Scrutiny Group**: This comprises of the Police Divisional Commander, the Chief Executive of Scottish Borders Council and the Chief Executive of NHS Borders. This is a very good model to provide overarching scrutiny of protection of vulnerable adults issues.

- **Management of the social work learning disability team**: The impressive work done by the manager of the social work learning disability team to bring together one team from different "factions" of social work and health staff.

- **Police Family Protection Unit model**: It is a robust, tried and tested model that stands up to scrutiny. It was notable that despite the introduction of tighter procedures throughout inter-agency partnership working there has not been a significant increase in the number of reported incidents to the police or the Fiscal. The co-location of officers in the Family Protection Unit alongside health and social work staff has greatly helped communication.

- **Commitment of elected members**: We met with elected members from Scottish Borders Council. They were all very committed to improving the quality of protection of vulnerable adult practice. They seemed to very aware of the issues.

- **Health improvement initiatives**: These initiatives and the multi-agency work done by the Chair of the new Primary and Community Services was a model of good practice, which should be disseminated widely.

- **Inter-agency work**: We liked the involvement of primary care staff in the Learning Disability Health Improvement Steering Group.

- **Health improvement strategy**: We were pleased to see the NHS Borders draft "Health Improvement Strategy for People with Learning Disabilities". This clearly acknowledged the importance of the "NHS Health Scotland Learning Disability Health Needs Assessment Report" and gave "proposed actions" for each of the Tiers 0-4.

- **The mental health team leader**: They provide quarterly peer supervision for all MHO's.

Operational level; staff and staffing

- **Inter-agency work apparent in social work case files**: The high level of involvement between social workers and other workers, including those who might have daily contact with people with learning disabilities, meant that social workers had up to date knowledge about most of them. This indirect work is important. It requires skill and judgement and deserves proper recognition.

- **Good record keeping**: Overall case records were up to date, clear, well organised, and well maintained. There was evidence of a flurry of scrutiny and activity prior to the review but in most cases, this was to ensure that work already done or underway was properly evidenced.

- **Good standard of administration**: All social work case files were well organised, allowing easy access to information contained therein.

- **Staff supervision records**: All staff were receiving regular supervision and there was a typed record of supervision sessions. Cases were reviewed regularly and "actions" to be taken by the social worker identified. Each worker had an annual Personal Professional Development Plan.

- **One case file included "practice advice reports"**: These were third party assessments of practice in cases where the procedure for protecting vulnerable adults had been invoked. This is a potentially useful aid to quality assurance, particularly in identifying good practice.

- **Education staff**: Strong committed and highly motivated individuals working in the education sector.

- **Inter-agency work**: Inclusive pre-school perspective and practice at one nursery.

- **Post school links**: Well-developed links with the Further Education college, further strengthened by the good practice processes developed by education and by the joint health, social work and educational psychology services paper on multi-agency procedures for transition from children to adult services. It would be helpful to draw these papers and procedures together to form one policy for all agencies to follow.

- **Police family protection unit**: This relies heavily on "information gathering and sharing". We asked the police representatives if information sharing has overcome perceived agency barriers. It now open and transparent, particularly for "out of hours incidents." There is a staffed twenty-four hour facility.

- **The mental health team and adults with incapacity unit**: They hold regular surgeries in local social work offices.

- **Outreach Team**: We were impressed with the multi-disciplinary intensive outreach team and how they supported parents with learning disabilities to look after potentially vulnerable new babies. The quality of the overall practice and the joint working was very high and this seemed like an excellent model of multi-disciplinary working.

- **Values based practice**: Staff we met had the values that people with learning disabilities should be treated with respect. They were very keen to show us the progress since the SWSI and Mental Welfare Commission reports were published, and there was a general enthusiasm for improvement.

- **New appointments**: We welcomed the appointments and work to date of a child health nurse consultant and a specialist dietician.

- **Pilot care co-ordination project**: This project in joint care planning for children with complex health care needs was impressive and showed promise for longer term use.

- **Joint work**: There was well planned and coordinated work being done between health promotion, dietetics and speech and language therapy in promoting healthy eating for teenagers with learning disabilities.

- **New dietetic assessment form**: The dietician has devised a form specifically for initial assessment of people with learning disabilities.

- **Emergency Duty Team (social work)**: One example of multi-disciplinary involvement was the social work emergency duty team covering all of the Borders. They reported frequent contact with health professionals at Borders General Hospital, duty GPs and learning disability services. Lists of adults with learning disabilities, vulnerable adults (including people with learning disabilities) appropriate adults and people subject to Guardianship orders were kept by the team. There was some sharing of this information with social work colleagues, but limited sharing with health staff.

- **Discharge liaison team**: At Borders General Hospital, the planning and inter-agency co-ordination through this team made sure that necessary support was in place for people with learning disabilities leaving hospital.

Protection of vulnerable adults with learning disabilities

- **Risk assessments**: We read files about some vulnerable people in extremely complex circumstances who were at risk of causing harm to themselves or others. In most of these cases, the vulnerable adults procedures had been followed. Thorough and thoughtful risk assessments had been carried out and there was ample evidence of co-operation with the relevant agencies. There had also been full and careful attention paid to the needs, views and feelings of people with learning disabilities and their families and good and continuing communication with them. In a few cases, the social work department had had to maintain the rights of individuals in the face of some community hostility. Reports were clear and well written. There was evidence of careful decision-making. Care plans were well constructed and adhered to. It appeared that the well-maintained and carefully monitored care packages were meeting the needs of individuals in the least restrictive circumstances compatible with their safety and the interests of other relevant people. Given the recent history which led to the inspection, social workers and their managers might have been tempted to be extremely cautious and make decisions as free of risk as possible. These might ensure safety but at the expense of individuals' rights and wishes. We thought that through thoughtful and thorough implementation of the vulnerable adults' procedures and good social work practice, a proper balance had been achieved.

- **Case file recording**: Reading of files generally revealed the social work service expending considerable effort in bringing its case recording up to an acceptable standard. In most cases – particularly vulnerable adult cases – significant progress appeared to have been made. Indeed, a high standard of case recording had been achieved in a small but significant number of case files.

- **Case file practice**: The case files demonstrated significant levels of inter-agency working – the greater the degree of vulnerability, the more prominent inter-agency working tended to feature. The efforts of one first line manager in particular in terms of auditing files and managing priorities, are worthy of note. Overall outcomes in vulnerable adult cases, particularly ensuring safety, were satisfactory. The social work department has a grip on cases, and has avoided "drifting". This good practice process was much stronger than previously reported to Scottish Borders Council elected members.

- **Looked after children**: There was more regular planning and review of cases when looked after children (LAC) were involved.

- **Good practice presentation**: In a presentation to the inspection team, we heard about some very thoughtful and effective work to support and protect vulnerable adults with learning disabilities. They were living in very difficult, complex circumstances.

- **Conscientious and well-motivated staff**: All of the staff we met were very shocked by the SWSI and Mental Welfare Commission investigations into the abuse of the vulnerable adults with learning disabilities in Borders. All staff were very conscientious and well motivated and keen to show the inspectors that the poor standard of practice identified (in the investigation reports) was not at all general in the social work department or NHS Borders.

- **Responsive Health Centre**: One health centre had a customised front sheet on case notes, showing if a person has a learning disability and/or is a vulnerable adult. The information was being well used by receptionists and others. For example, when a person phoned or called for an appointment, consideration could be given to a suitable time, or to a double slot for an appointment to allow more time.

- **Toolkit for Vulnerable Adults**: Primary and community services had developed a training and reference resource to raise awareness and improve levels of protection.

Meeting practical needs and improving people's quality of life

- **Awareness of peoples rights and wishes**: This is very much connected with protection and risk management. The case files showed careful work, involving some risk, but undertaken in the light of peoples rights and wishes and with all appropriate safeguards in place. During the inspection, people told us how much they wanted independence. There could have been a danger of completely avoidance of risk following the incidents which led up to the enquiry. This does not seem to have happened.

- **Flexibile care plans**: Several case files showed much liaison within the social work department and with other agencies to ensure care packages which supported people's social activity. Workers seemed to have reasonable freedom to set up such arrangements and some showed considerable ingenuity in maximising people's resources and community contacts.

- **People in their own houses**: In Scottish Borders, there is a threefold increase in the numbers of people with learning disabilities living independently in their own tenancies. People that we met with were very proud to show us their new homes, and tenants had good relationships with the staff who supported them.

- **Bright New Futures**: This initiative was at early stages, but had high potential for promoting integrated working. It is a multi-agency strategy for children and young people in the Scottish Borders. It has been developed in partnership with Education, the Scottish Children's Reporters Administration, Lothian & Borders Police, the local voluntary sector, NHS Borders and the social work department.

- **Flexible responses in education**: There was a flexible response to the needs of pupils with learning disabilities. For example, the appointment of a primary trained teacher bringing a different range of teaching approaches to support pupils with learning disabilities within secondary schools.

- **Parents of pupils with learning disabilities**: They mentioned good support for young carers.

- **Involvement in meetings**: Lots of people with learning disabilities attended many of the meetings. There was particularly good attendance at the session on involving people with learning disabilities. People who attended meetings were very comfortable, confident and well supported. People with learning disabilities led some of the sessions at meetings and were well supported to do this. They seemed to have a very good relationship with their support workers.

- **Briefing for interviews**: Most of the people with learning disabilities who were interviewed as part of the inspection were well briefed before the interview by their social workers or other staff.

- **Campaigning family carers**: Relatives of people with learning disabilities played a crucial role in getting the carers supported accommodation off the ground. They persevered despite setbacks, to deliver an excellent resource for people with learning disabilities.

- **Respite for children**: We were impressed with the respite house for children with learning disabilities. The parents we met were all very satisfied with the service they and their children get.

The Scottish Consortium for Learning Disability survey of people with learning disabilities and family carers in the Borders.

scottish
consortium
for learning
disability

Building respect in the
Scottish community

The Borders Independent Advocacy Service (BIAS) conducted the interviews for the survey.

A person with learning disabilities living in Scottish Borders, 2005 told us:

> "No fears as long as we all work together. It will get better as we keep thinking about what we want".

Report of interviews in the Scottish Borders

Methods

The Social Work Inspection Agency commissioned some additional interviews as part of the Joint Inspection in Scottish Borders. A topic guide was designed by the Scottish Consortium for Learning Disability after consultation with People First Scotland. The topic guide was approved by the Joint Inspection Steering Group. It was a version of the questionnaire that was later shortened for use by the inspectors.

The purpose of the questionnaire was to ascertain the views of some people with learning disabilities about the support they received. There was a particular emphasis on choice, speaking up and safety. The questionnaire also considered whether people's lives were changing and how they felt about their quality of life, including their opportunities to make friends and have new experiences.

The target sample size was 20 (including five children and young people).

Samples

Twenty interviews were conducted by two interviewers from BIAS. Two of the people interviewed were family carers and 14 were with adults with learning disabilities. Four young people with learning disabilities (aged approx 16) also completed an activity as part of the research. They attended a learning support unit.

The services through which individuals were identified are shown in Table 1. Four separate day services, two of which were in the independent sector, identified adults for interview. Other interviewees were identified through two residential services and a workshop. We are grateful to managers and staff for their support for the work.

We would like to thank all those who spoke to us about themselves. We will prepare an accessible summary of the report.

The table also shows the range of living arrangements represented in the sample. Of the 14:

- Four lived in residential care;

- Five lived in the family home; and

- Five lived in their own tenancies/supported living.

Two people were on the verge of a major transition as their residential unit was closing. Where other services received were mentioned at interview, these are also shown.

It had been agreed that demographic information (age, gender, and ethnicity) would not be recorded for reasons of confidentiality. However it can be confirmed that that the twelve adults included people of both genders and of a wide range of ages.

Table 1   **Interview sample**

Accessed through	Other services	Living arrangements	Employment	Interviewer
Day centre 1		Lives on own		A
Day centre 1	Home support – independent provider	Lives on own	Has worked for 10 years, part time	A
Day centre 1	Home support – independent provider	Lives on own		B
Day centre 1		Lives on own		B
Day centre 2	Care worker	Family home		A
Day centre 2	Support worker	Family home		A
Day centre 3		Family home	Works part time	A
Workshop		Lives on own, sheltered housing		A
Day centre 4	College	Family home	Works part time	B
Day centre 4	Learning disability team	Family home	Works	B
Residential service 1		Large residential service		A
Residential service 1		Large residential service		A
Residential unit 2	Day centre 5	Unit is closing	Wants a job	B

Residential unit 2	Day centre 5	Unit is closing		B
Carer		Family home, adult son with learning disabilities who attends day centre		A
Carer		Lives with son (young man in transition)		B
Learning support unit		Family home		B
Learning support unit		Family home		B
Learning support unit		Family home		B
Learning support unit		Family home		B

Findings

For each set of questions the questions asked will be listed and then the numbers of responses will be shown, followed by comments made by the people interviewed. Information which might identify people has been removed wherever possible from the comments. Results will be reported first for the fourteen adults with learning disabilities, then for the family carers and finally the young people.

Interviewer A had a higher proportion of people who answered only 'yes' or 'no' to many questions. The people spoken to by interviewer B generally made more comments, enabling her to use the topic guide format for the interview. However as a result there are more 'no responses' in these interviews.

A 'no' response may indicate either that the question was not asked or that it was not answered. A 'yes' or 'no' answer has only been inferred when it was clearly intended by the person comment[1].

Adults with learning disabilities (n = 14)

The support you get

This section asked about the relationship with support workers, satisfaction with support received and choice. It builds on work that has asked people 'what makes a good worker'.

Do you trust the people who support you?

- Do you have a say in who supports you?
- Do the people who support you take the time with you that you need?

---
[1] Any inferred response is shown in brackets in the Access data report.

- Do you feel that the people who support you really care about you?
- Do you feel that the people who support you respect you for who you are?

Chart 1   Support: responses

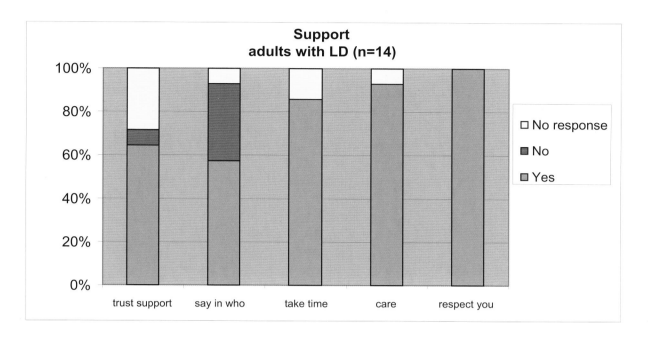

Table 2   Support: comments

Trust support	*(yes) … (provider) comes in the evening. ..(worker's name) is in the office. All the staff are nice.*
	(yes) I feel well respected here and lucky to have got what I have got.
Say in support	*(yes) Social worker is very helpful. I know how to phone him where he works.*
	(no) Very nice staff. I need physical support. I don't choose staff or keyworker.
	No I work every morning on the phones and reception with … (name)
Take time	*(yes) sometimes … (name of service user) phones to find out where they are. They go to her next.*
Care	*(yes) I get … (names of three workers)… (another worker) comes fortnightly for a chat from the office.*
	(yes) They respect our views.
	(yes) I have a better relationship with staff now than I have ever had.
Respect	*(yes) I go out with … (name of worker) every two weeks for the afternoon. Selkirk glass is very nice but very expensive!*
	Yes brought in 'Hitch' for us to watch on DVD when I asked.
	(yes) … (name of day centre manager) is good. She is great to talk to. Has made good changes. Good respect.
	Yes I feel treated as an equal with staff. I get information on any changes from my manager.

This section suggests that relationships with staff were good. The comments provide some detail that bears this out. The person who replied 'no' to the question about trust answered all the other questions positively. However five people reported that they had no say in the people who supported them.

Can you make choices and decisions about the things that are important to you?

Do you get the:

- information;
- support; and
- any communication support you need to help you with this?

Chart 2   Support for choices: responses

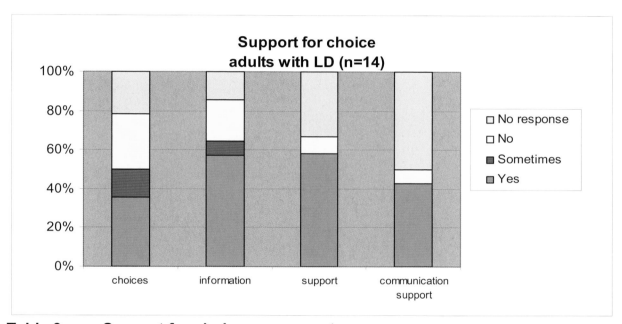

Table 3   Support for choices: comments

Choices	*(no) There was no choice only ...(name of residential unit).*
	I sometimes feel that I am being pushed to work in a real office, but I want to be confident. I have looked at 'ways to work' who are trying to find the right place. I do feel more confident to get work outside with their help.
Information	*(no) I need more information about the move to ... (name of place). We have not had much so far.*
	Yes my support staff and family help. I hope my new social worker is better than the last one.
	(no) I wanted to choose gardening. I missed the opportunity.

Responses on choice were much more evenly balanced suggesting that this is more of an issue. A couple of respondent comments indicated that some people were willing to make critical comments where they felt this was justified. Unfortunately the questionnaires do not identify whether communication support was required by any of these individuals. All took part in interviews without it.

Can you get support to live the kind of life you want to lead?

- Do you get the kind of support you want?
- Do you get the amount of support you want?
- Can you get your support when you want it?
- Do the people who support you know how to help you get the kind of opportunities you want?

Chart 3   Support for life you want: responses

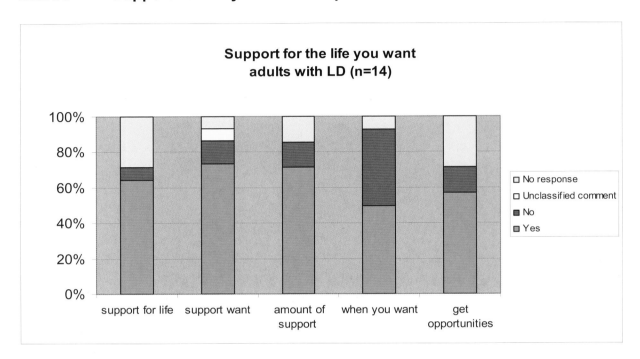

Table 4   Support for life you want: comments

Support for life	*(no) I choose activities at … (name of day centre), listening to CDs in the sensory room for an hour. I would like the satisfaction of something to do during the day, that's all that matters.*
	(yes) I plan my own timetable at … (name of day centre).
	(yes) I have been to college two times to do computers. I work at … (name of shop) on a … (day of week). The staff are excellent. I want to stick to …(name of shop) and … (name of day centre) and not join ways to work. I go to the library to look up the internet for cheats for Play station 2.
	I have my car, (family) and the best sister-in-law in Scotland. I can phone any of them up on a Saturday and say 'what are you up to and where are we going?'
Support want	*(yes) My social worker helps with my finances.*
	(no) I would like to do a job but I need confidence.

	(no) I don't get individual support. (no) – I do History group. Have a wander round here to find a person to do things.
Amount of support	(yes) The amount I get is fine. (no) I don't go out in the evenings.
When you want	(no) It depends on the staff. It is isolated here. (no) Can't choose by myself, have to go with the groups. (no) Carer comes to suit her.
Get opportunities	(no) I have never been offered the chance of a job. (no) I would love to go horse riding again. I have never had the time to speak to … (name) about it. I go independently to visit my family in … (name of place). I like my house and know the buses. I email my family on … (name of country).

Most people said that they were getting the support to live the kind of life they wanted as well as the type and amount of support they wanted. There was greater dissatisfaction with the timing of support. One person felt he had a chance to make choices at the day centre but answered no to all the other questions in this section because he felt he was not getting support to get a job which was what he most wanted. The other resident in that unit also spoke of the social isolation she experienced. There were two examples of support tailored to the person – help with finances and a reduction in support at a time when it had not been wanted. The comments show that there were people who wanted more appropriate support to access the opportunities that they wanted.

Having a say

This section asked about people's access to having a say including copies of their care plans, support at reviews, access to complaints, access to advocacy and the chance to get involved in changing things.

Can you say if you do not like something about your service?

- Do you have a copy of your care plan or personal life plan?
- Do you go to review meetings? Do you get support there? Are you listened to?
- Do you know how to make a complaint?
- Have you ever complained?
- What happened?

Chart 4   Able to say if you do not like your service: responses

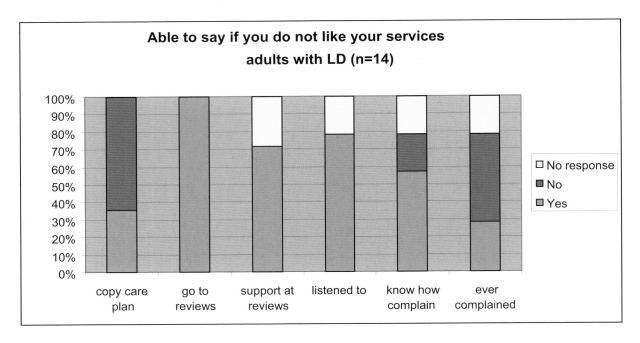

Able to say if you do not like your services
adults with LD (n=14)

Legend:
- □ No response
- ■ No
- ■ Yes

Categories: copy care plan, go to reviews, support at reviews, listened to, know how complain, ever complained

Table 5   Able to say if you do not like your service: comments

Copy care plan	(no) Kept at centre. (no) Not aware of care plan. (no)Thistle Foundation did a person centred plan a long time ago. I don't know where it is now.
Listened to	(yes) My four hours support on a Saturday was too much and it stopped. I have more independence now.
Know how complain	(no) Not aware of complaints about staff but they are all nice. I would report the bossy one to ... (name) or ... (name) at the day centre.
Ever complained	(yes) To support worker when neighbour kept banging on window. Satisfactorily resolved. (yes) I complained to Scottish Power about a letter. They said I owed ... (lot of money). My social worker sorted it out. (yes) I was in a shared room. I now have my own room but share when people come in for respite. (yes) I complained about a staff member not showing up. She was a problem and has left.

More people did not have a copy of their care plan than had one. Some people knew that a plan was kept at the day centre. One person in residential care had had a person-centred plan but did not know what had happened to it. Personal life plans or person-centred plans might help address mismatch between aspirations and support.

Reviews were reported on favourably. Everyone went to their review and most felt supported and listened to. There was one example of a change resulting from a review which the person felt had increased her independence.

It is of concern that three people said that they did not know how to make a complaint. On the other hand four had done so and gave details of the important change that had resulted for them. Three of these had some involvement in/access to advocacy.

Do you have a say in how your service is run?

- Are you asked what you think about the services you use?
- How is this done?
- Do you think that what you say is listened to?
- Is there a residents' or members' committee in your service?
- Do managers and staff listen to what the committee says?
- Do people on the committee get the support they need to take part?
- Does the committee get support from any one who is independent of the service?
- Has the committee ever got something changed? Tell us about this
- Have you ever been on the committee?
- Did you feel that you could have your say on it?

Chart 5   Having a say: responses

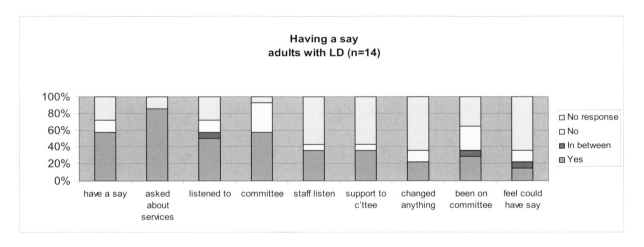

Table 6   Having a say: comments

Have a say	(yes) I have been to … with (name of manager) to find out about day supports. In (other area) centres are 'outposts'. A good idea. Part of the Finding Out project.
	(yes) On Interest Link Committee.
Asked about services	(yes) I am coming back from … (day centre) early tomorrow as Scottish Borders Council are coming to talk about the new building.
How asked	Team meeting
	Service users' committee

	Members' group
Listened to	*(yes) They ask us about colours for the new building, what activities should be on during the day.* *(yes) We were asked about choices for lunches and asked all the others, helped with planning and colours for the extension.*
Committee	*(yes) I am on the committee at the day centre.* *(yes) I can speak up at the resident's committee.*
Staff listen	*(yes) I feel more involved, not shut off and it's more open.*
Changed anything	*(I don't know) – we ask questions about the move with SBC rep.* *(yes) – they asked us about the new building.*
Feel could have say	*(yes) I can speak up.* *Sometimes on the … (day centre) committee.*

Most people said there were asked about the services they received, usually through regular meetings and eight said they had some say in how services were run. They do seem to be formal mechanisms for consultation but the results suggest that regular, everyday involvement of individuals in decision-making and opportunities to speak up could be further developed.

Do you have an advocate?

- If not, do you want one?
- Do you know what advocacy is?
- Do you know how to get an advocate if you need one?
- Do you go to an advocacy group?

Chart 6   Advocacy: responses

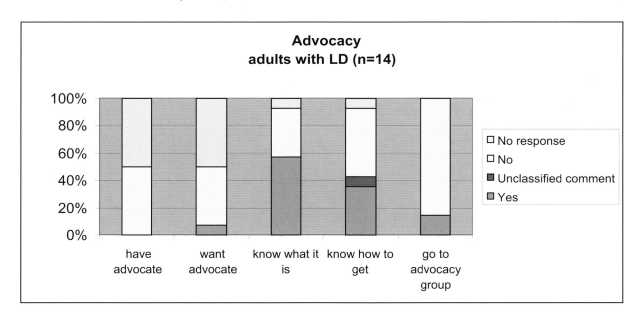

Table 7   **Advocacy: comments**

Know what it is	*(yes) Know what advocacy is because of People First.*
Know how to get	*Mum and dad speak up for me.* *(yes) at … (name of advocacy organisation).* *Don't need one. I would go to … (name of day centre manager) or … (name of social worker).*
Go to advocacy group	*(yes) People First. At the conference we speak to politicians and council leaders.* *(no) Nobody has asked me about People First. … (name) might tell me if I can go with one of the staff – might give me a lift.* *(no) It happens at a bad time for me. I don't want to.* *(no) Do not want to go. I know how to speak up for myself.* *(no) I have been a couple of times to People First but it usually doubles up with my planning day.*

None of those interviewed had an advocate and only one person expressed a wish for one. However two people were taking part in collective advocacy. Awareness of advocacy seems to have come from advocacy organisations themselves, People First and BIAS. Some people said that they felt able to speak for themselves. There is room to increase the awareness of what advocacy is and how to get an advocate. Five people did not know what advocacy was and seven people said that they did not know how to contact an advocate.

Do you get a chance to help change things?

- Tell us about your experiences
- Is there anyone who helps you to speak up?
- Have you had any training or support in speaking up?
- Have you ever been involved in changing services, for example a planning group?
- Have you got involved in changing things in your community?
- If you don't like anything, what stops you from changing it?
- What would help you have a bigger say?

Chart 7   Change things: responses

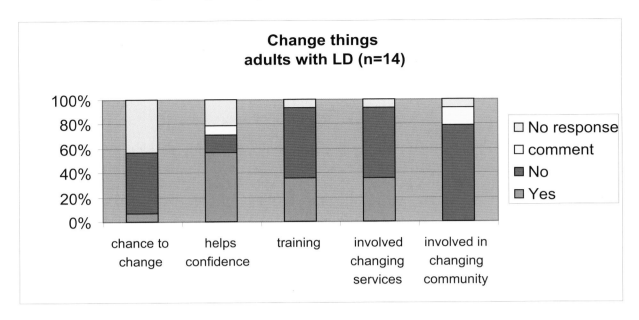

Table 8   Change things: comments

Chance to change	(no) – lunches stopped with no say. (yes) I 'm part of the Finding Out project. We want to make day services better.
Help to have confidence	(yes) The manager, my mum, my physio. I feel confident to speak to people I know.
Training	(no) But would be interested in some. (yes) I am on the SCLD team. (yes) Interviewing for new staff before they go on to the next panel. (yes) Have had opportunity to interview new staff.
Involved changing services	I was involved in the Quality Network Services Review. … (name) is supporting me with paperwork and transport. I was a presenter at a staff training day using PowerPoint. (yes) I enjoy going to conferences, training and helping at interviews.
Involved in changing community	Involved in the church. I have been to Lourdes. But I spoke to Father … (name) to complain about the prices and the church go there every year. We should have a change. …. (name) week. I help at the craft stall when children's school sports are on the playing field behind the centre.
What stops you	Difficulty understanding. Bit frightened. Not allowed.

Help bigger say	*Training.*
	Advocate.
	More confidence.
	To be able to speak up.

More than half of those interviewed could identify someone who helped them to have confidence. Only one person said they had had a chance to change things, although five people did say they had had an opportunity to get involved in something like a planning group. There were some strong examples of participation (training, interviewing, quality reviews) as well as an example of not being consulted (lunches stopped without consultation). One person said that they were "not allowed" to change things they did not like. There were five suggestions of how people felt that their opportunity to contribute could be improved. There is scope for building on work already done to increase participation. For those already involved, the experience has apparently been very positive.

Your social worker

This section asked whether the person had a social worker and their experience of them. It particularly explores trust and protection. It builds on the work of the User and Carer Panel for the 21st Century Social Work Review as well as the recommendations from the SWSI and Mental Welfare Commission reports (May 2004).

Do you have a social worker?

- Where do they work?
- When did you last see them?
- Could you meet with them on your own?
- Did they explain things well to you?
- Did they give you the information you need?
- Do they take the time to listen to you?
- Do they understand what you really need?
- Do you trust them to help you make the decisions that are best for you?
- Do you feel that they know you as a person?
- Do you feel they are on your side?
- Are they able to make things happen for you?
- Do they know enough about any other services that you are involved with?
- Do you think they can get action by other people when necessary? (health services, education etc)
- If something bad happened:
    - Would you tell them?
    - Would they find out anyway?
    - Would they be able to do anything to protect you?

Chart 8a Social worker: responses

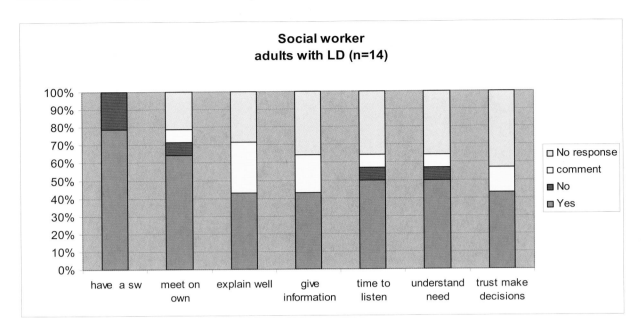

Chart 8b Social worker: responses

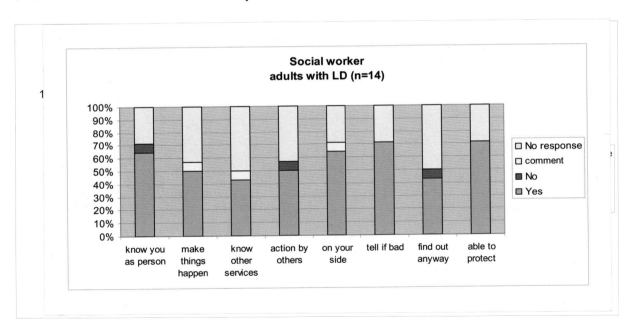

Table 9 Social worker: comments

Have a social worker	Yes – several different over the years.
	No. I had … (name) about 11 years ago from … (name of place). No one since he left.
When last seen	Last week.
	A couple of months ago.

	December 2004. Social worker was sick for March review.
	She comes for my six monthly reviews.
	She comes to the meetings about the new building.
Meet on own	*(yes) Haven't but could.*
	Yes I would get in touch by phone if I had any worries.
Explain well	*Sometimes.*
	Too new to tell but seems nice.
Give information	*Sometimes.*
	(yes) She got information.
Time to listen	*She's new. We've only had a couple of meetings.*
Understand need	*no, mother understands.* *She wants to arrange a review to get to know me better.*
Trust make decisions	*Most of the time.* *Not yet.*
Make things happen	*She is helpful. She got me into … (name of centre).* *(no social worker) I am happy with … (name of day centre) and … (name of where works). I do not want to make any changes. I went to … (name of provider) respite twice a long time ago after high school. A good way to get away from work/home is a two week holiday.* *(yes) If I'm not happy with something I would tell her. I have no worries at the moment. I feel confident that it would be straightforward. If I complained change would happen.*
Action by others	*Yes, work shops, weaving, wood work.* *yes – health.*
On your side	*The last social worker had no time. I only saw them twice. They were no help during my … (name of operation). From October to January I had no one.* *Yes we have a good relationship.*
Tell if bad	*Yes always.*
Able to protect	*Yes – get police.*

Eleven of the 14 respondents had a social worker and three said they did not. On questions relating to protection the responses were positive. Of the 11, nine people said they could meet their social worker on their own, 10 that they would tell their social worker if something bad happened (no one said that they could not tell them) and ten that they believed that their social worker would be able to protect them. It is positive that nine people said that they felt their social worker was on their side (one did not) and that nine felt their social worker really knew them as a person (again one person said they did not). Most (seven) felt that their social worker could make things happen. One negative experience was reported and one person said that their mother rather than their social worker understood their needs.

Feeling safe

This section focused on safety from the perspective of the person with learning disabilities. It asked whether there is someone they could tell if frightened, how safe they feel when out and about and what would help them to feel safe.

If you were worried or frightened is there someone you could tell?

- Would you be able to contact them quickly?
- Would you be able to speak to them in private?
- Do you think people would believe someone if they said they were being hurt?
- Mental Welfare Commission? Heard of? Know what they do? Know how to contact?
- Care Commission? Heard of? Know what they do? Know how to contact?

Chart 9   Feeling safe: responses

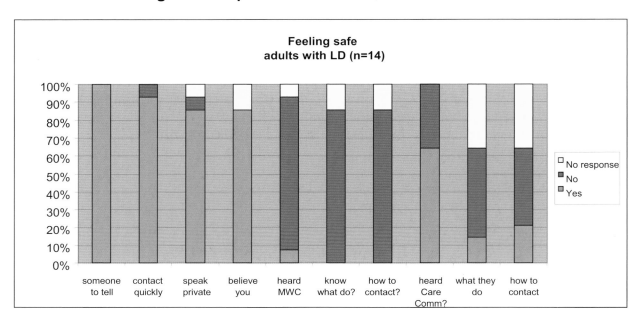

Table 10   Feeling safe: comments

Someone to tell	*(yes) Mum, key-worker. I felt bullied a long time ago. I had a word with my key-worker and they passed it on to mum and it was fine after that.*
	... (name of provider), (name of social worker) when I get to know her better, my friend lives nearby.
	(yes) Police – I would get support from my mother, father, brothers and the staff team.
Contact quickly	*See person at day centre every day.*
Speak private	*Yes, ... (name of day centre manager) or key worker if I had suspicions of bullying.*

	No, other member of staff present.
Believe you	*Yes, the staff are all good.*
	Yes, have in the past and it was sorted.
	Staff may not, but other people would e.g. social worker.
Heard of MWC	*Yes, are you still allowed to say mental and call them that. Is that not cheeky?*
Heard Care Commission?	*Yes, they come round.*
	Yes … (name) was talking about them at … (name of day centre).
What they do	*Yes,….was in here last week to see us.*
How to contact	*(yes) … (name) was here last week. His phone number is on the wall. I told him how good the day service had been when I was in hospital.*

Everyone interviewed said that they knew someone they could tell if they were worried or frightened and all but one person could contact them quickly. Staff and family were the people most often identified for this. Twelve of the 14 people said that people would be believed if they said they were being hurt and one person evidenced this from experience. One person felt that the social worker was more likely to believe it than were staff.

By contrast, there was very low recognition of the Mental Welfare Commission. Twelve people had never heard of it. There had been recent contact about the Care Commission and nine people were aware of it, but only three people said they would know how to make contact.

3.4.2 How safe do you feel if you are out and about?

- Street?
- Transport?
- Places you visit?
- Do people get picked on or called names in your area?

Chart 10   Out and about: responses

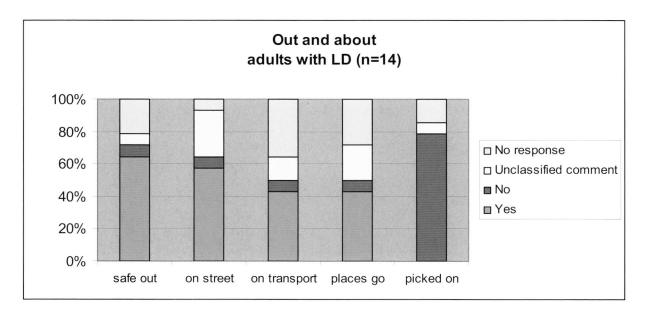

Table 11   Out and about: comments

Safe out	OK carry an alarm in handbag.
	I do feel safe on routes I know. I know how to phone 999.
	Mum helps me with road safety. I have lots of schoolmates around.
	Attitudes are changing. I feel safe anywhere. I have loads of pals in … (name of place). For my birthday I filled the hall with my friends (all of them able-bodied). My mother did not believe I knew so many people. They just see me as me.
	OK phones … (provider) every night at 9pm. Also caries an alarm.
	Frightened to go out by self, OK with family and staff.
On street	I am confident in … (name of place) in the street.
	A long time ago a bloke was cheeky about my crutches just when I was getting out of my wheelchair first. My brother had a word with him. I have never had any bother since.
	Not if there are cars.
	We did road safety training through the day centre with an officer from the police.
	As a wheelchair user I sometimes feel worried because of wobbly pavements.
On transport	OK in centre minibus with escort, frightened on public transport.
	Not on bus.
	Yes goes home to parent's home town on own by public transport.
Places go	Only with other people.
	Yes with staff – pub, on outings.
	I always watch my bag and keep my money safe.

Although nine people said that they felt safe out and about, the comments showed variation in the extent to which people felt comfortable in the street or on transport. Some could manage alone, others only with support. Some good safety strategies were identified including alarms and road safety training. Name – calling was definitely not identified as an issue. The replies showed the importance of support to people feeling able to get around and the varied levels of comfort and independence in travelling.

3.4.3 What would help you to feel safe?

- What might stop someone saying they were frightened?
- Place?
- Person?
- Procedure?

Table 12   Help to feel safe: responses

	Answer	No answer
Help feel safe	10	4
Stop from saying	4	10

Table 13   help to feel safe: comments

Help feel safe	*I stay in well lit places in the evenings.* *Feels safe with people and in places knows.* *I take my alarm with me if I go out at night. I bought it myself from the police station. I have a smoke alarm and a Border Care alarm in the house.* *I always go out with staff.*
Stop from saying	*If can't speak.* *If they could not speak up like me.* *I don't feel happy. I'm a bit nervous when I go on a journey for the first time.* *What might happen but would always tell if frightened.*

Ten people suggested 14 things that would help them feel safe. The biggest category comprised other people. Technology was also identified including alarms and mobile phones. One person kept to well lit areas at night.

Your health

Do you get the information you need to lead a healthy life?

- Food
- Staying active
- Medicines

If you are worried about your health, is there anyone you can speak to?

- Family
- Friend
- Key worker

- Support worker
- GP
- Nurse
- Other

Chart 11   Your health: responses

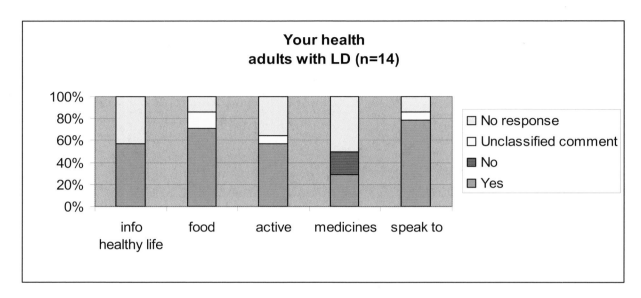

**Your health
adults with LD (n=14)**

Legend:
☐ No response
☐ Unclassified comment
■ No
■ Yes

X-axis: info healthy life, food, active, medicines, speak to

Table 14   Your health: comments

Info healthy life	LD team physiotherapist
Food information	*Understand healthy eating.* *Yes, helps in kitchen.* *Cookery classes.* *I am a smoker, it is controlled to 10 roll-ups a day. I went on a diet last year and now I am happy that my* *Yes I have … (chronic illness) and partial vision.*
Stay active information	*Take exercise.* *Likes to walk.* *Swim weekly.* *Yes, likes dancing.* *In wheelchair.*
Medicine information	*Take as told.* *Understands about taking regularly.*
Speak if worried	*If I was worried I would speak to…or my friend….* *Worried about access to the doctor when I move.*

Who to speak to	*Key-worker.*
	All except nurses
	Social worker or friend
	Dietician,
	Physio, I get lots of support from … (name of member of LD Team)

Eleven people identified at least one person they could talk to if they were worried about their health, although one person was concerned about possible access to the doctor after moving to a new house. Comments were more about health behaviour than information but showed an awareness of healthy lifestyles.

3.5.2 Your doctor

- Do they take the time you need?
- Can you have a supporter with you?
- Do they understand your needs?
- Do they get you the help you need?

Chart 12   Doctor: responses

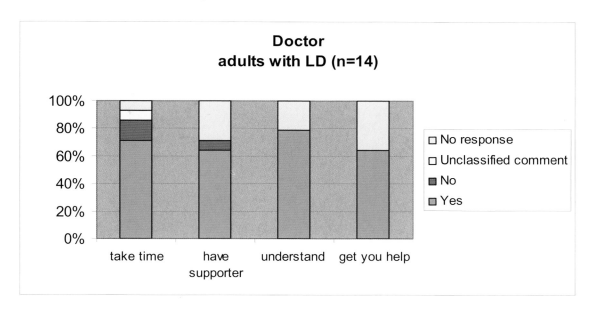

Table 15   Doctor: comments

Doctor takes time	*No felt rushed.*
	I would go to all the GPs, they are all nice.
	I saw the skin specialist at the doctor's in … (name of place). For red blotches in summer. I got good information on cream. I felt very comfortable. He was calm and kept me calm.

	Yes very good, consultant very good. *(yes) He tells you now. He used to tell your mother.* *Doctor … (name) comes to … (the unit). Worried that new doctor will not come to new house.*

The responses about doctors were positive with 11 people reporting that the doctor understood their needs and only two saying they felt rushed, as compared with two who did not. Two people gave favourable accounts of specialists. One person was pleased that the doctor now spoke to him instead of to his mother, as in the past.

3.5.3 Your nurse

- Do you see a nurse?
- Do they take the time you need?
- Do they give you useful information?
- Can they get you the help you need for your health?

Chart 13   Nurse: responses

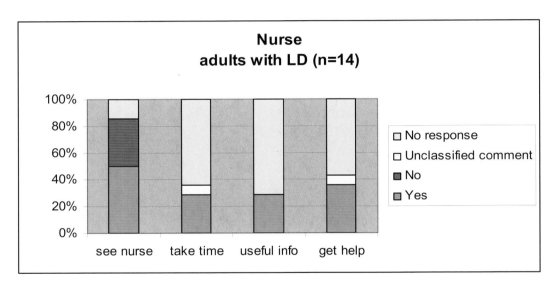

Table 16   Nurse: comments

See nurse	*I go for a mammogram check-up.* *I had tests done. I was treated with respect. My nurse is married to my pal.*
Nurse takes time	*Yes, good follow-up.*

Fewer people (seven) reported seeing a nurse. The limited number of comments was positive.

In hospital

- Have you been into hospital recently?
- Did you feel that you were treated with respect?
- Did the doctors and nurses explain to you what was happening?
- Were you treated well or badly?
- Why do you say this?
- When you left hospital, did you know what to do to look after yourself?

Chart 14   Hospital: responses

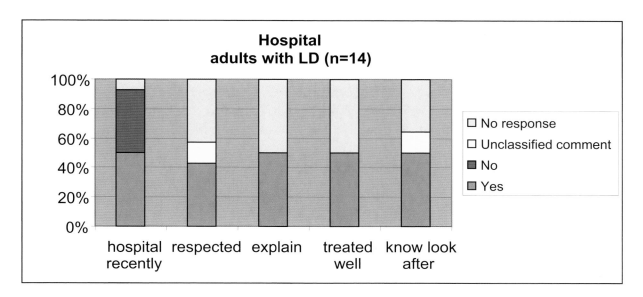

Table 17   Hospital: comments

In hospital recently?	Yes, I had a rash that was not clearing up. I had to go to the BGH to get antibiotics on a drip. I felt alright and knew they would help.
Treated with respect?	I have not been in recently, they were all very nice when I had to go in for my eye operation. I went for an eye test to the optician, phoned GP and went right away. I was sent to the Western and had to stay in for 6 weeks. … (name of day centre manager) drove me to… (name of place) to be with my family. Social workers were not around. I would have been stuck without the day service. … (names of workers) visited every night. … (name of social worker) wanted me to stay and get support from… (provider) but I complained.
Treated well	Well but did not like being moved from department to have tests carried out (out patient). Yes I was their friend. I was in BGH for tests. The BGH is getting better (food is good). The nurse from (where lives) came across with me, not as far as

	the ward. The nurse there explained the drip.
Did you know what to do when you left hospital?	I hurt my wrist and my social worker got me into respite at ARK. Yes (staff organised carer before she went home).

Seven people had been in hospital recently and all reported that they had been treated well. Six said they had felt respected. One person had attended outpatients and felt they had had to move around too much for tests. One person had experienced a lack of social work input when they were ill, although the staff of their day service had stepped in. There were examples of good information-giving and follow-up.

Your life

About the place you live in

- Are you comfortable or uncomfortable where you live?
- Do you get on with the people you live with?
- If you wanted to move, do you think you would be able to do so?

Chart 15   The place you live: responses

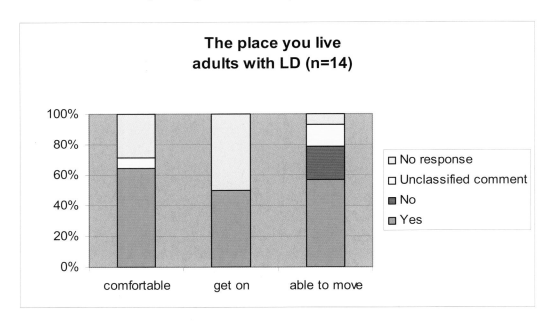

Table 18   The place you live: comments

Comfortable or not comfortable?	Very comfortable (lives alone). Would like to move to house with no stairs (in process).
Get on with the people I live with	I live alone. (yes) The residents are okay. (yes) Mum and dad. I'm happy living at home. It's the centre for my brothers.

Would you be able to move if you wanted to?	*Mum wants me to live at home.*
	All my friends live in Borders. I would not want to move back to ... (name of place).
	I had to move in 2001 because of noisy neighbours. I was fed up with the noise and the police had to sort it out.

Most people said that they were comfortable where they lived. Nine of the 10 people who lived with others said that they got on with them. Two were going to move to newly built property as their existing unit was closing. Three people said they would not be able to move if they wanted to.

About the people you know

- Do you have people in your life you can share things with?
- Do you know anyone who shares your interests?
- Is there anyone who helps you to go to places (new places and places you like already)?
- Is there anyone who helps you to feel safe?
- Is there anyone who helps you to be independent?
- Are you friendly with anyone who is not one of your support staff?
- Do you have a partner?

Chart 16   The people you know: responses

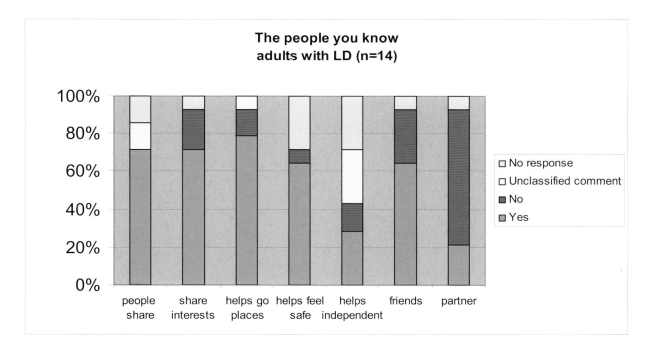

Table 19   The people you know: comments

People you can share things with	*(yes) I have a very positive attitude. Since I was 17 I have always wanted an office job, respect and opportunities. It has taken a long time to get here (respondent is in 40's). My job means so much to me.*

	Yes, friends, sports coach. Yes, care worker – bird watching.
Do you know anyone who shares your interests?	I go to a restaurant with a friend. I don't have friends outside. I don't do churches, I have school friends at … (name of day centre). Yes, sports friends. … (name) and … (name) are my friends I go and see. … (another name) sometimes blows hot and cold.
Help to go places	(yes) Retired staff – went to London with them, stayed in a hotel, west end shows, saw the sights. I watch SRV rugby on TV. Don't go to watch … (local team) play. No, we do most things as a group. I went to Kelso races and want to do more new things. Staff need a week's notice. I go out with … one a fortnight to go for a coffee. We go to different places.
Help you feel safe	(no). I am not allowed to go swimming or to the beach because I am vulnerable. Mum would be worried.
Helps you be independent	I am mostly independent. I go to People 1st. Able to maintain independence myself. Quite independent. Can go out and about by myself and look after own money. I am very aware of my disability. I will be independent when mum takes me out to see family or with her women friends. I have my own car but don't go out in it often – no staff.
Friendly with anyone not support staff	Yes, female resident. Yes, sports coach. Yes, family friend. … (name) is an old neighbour. I go to her new house. I go to church every Sunday.
Partner	No, if the right person came along that would be OK. I would look for someone with similar interests. No, but I'm always on the look out for romance.

	Boyfriend at centre.
	A male friend comes in for monthly respite. I would like to keep in touch after the move.

Most people were able to identify people and meaningful activities in their lives, although few identified a partner. Sports and work provided opportunities for friendships. However there were some people whose opportunities and networks were very restricted. One person was quite restricted at home, four had no friends except staff. One person was hoping that the planned move would not disrupt a relationship.

3.6.3 About the things you do and the opportunities you get

- Do you get the chance to lead the life you want to?
- Tell us what a good day is like for you.
- Tell us what a bad day is like for you.

Chart 17   **Things you do: responses**

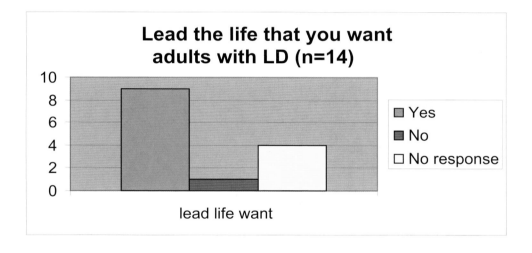

Table 20   Things you do: comments

Life you want	Yes, as well as attending the centre, several interests and very involved in sport. I go to cooking classes at college. … (name) has a very good group. Numeracy and reading also. No, I used to enjoy wheelchair sports, javelin, discus, shot. I enjoyed riding and drama. I love trains and planes.
Good day	I am very happy most days. Video games then a family night out. I like hot Saturdays on the back patio. Going to work, shops, out and about. Every day is good because they are all different.
Bad day	I never have a bad day. Not many bad days. Wednesday – the weather. When pain is bad. Not good when someone is annoying.

Only one person reported not being able to lead the life they wanted and that person spoke strongly of the things that they used to enjoy doing. There were some vivid descriptions of good days and very few reports of bad days, except for two people in regular pain. It is hard to interpret this. It might mean that people are contented or that they live one day at a time.

3.6.4 About how things have been lately

- What has been the biggest change in your life recently?
- Was it a change for the better or a change for the worse?
- Have you had any help with this?

Chart 18   Changes: responses

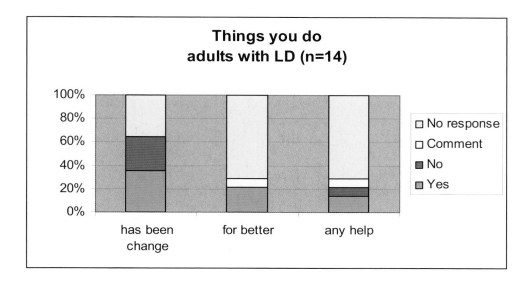

Tables 21   Changes: comments

Change	*Being able to do things for herself – cooking, housework.* *Moving to own home.* *Father died.* *Working.* *Will be moving.*
Better or worse	*I have many questions but I am looking forward to the move.*
Help with change	*Centre staff.* *Friend.* *Meeting council staff tomorrow. Have seen plans (of new house).*

Five major life changes were reported including two people moving into more independent living and one person starting work.

3.6.5 About your hopes and fears

- What is your biggest worry for the future?
- What is your biggest hope for the future?

Table 22   Hopes and fears: responses

	Answer	No answer
Biggest worry	13	1
Biggest hope	13	1

Table 23   Hopes and fears: comments

Biggest worry	*No fears as long as we all work together. It will get better as we keep thinking about what we want.*
	Don't have one. I would go to my key-worker or social worker.
	Being left alone.
	If anything happened to mother.
	Services will not be there.
	Will lack money stop my support.
Biggest hope	*To live independently.*
	Get married.
	To support (name of day centre) to have more events and to help out more there.
	To win a medal at the Olympics.
	To work full-time.
	To stay healthy.
	My family will come and visit more when I live in … (name of place).
	New building up in time and staff are good.
	Things have got easier as I've got older and this will continue. I am paying to hire a horse to go to the ride out. They don't ask for much and what are uncles for?

Six said they had no real worries. Two people feared being left alone and two people were concerned about whether their service would be sustained in the future.

Some of the same aspirations were shared by everyone (marriage, working remaining healthy). Other reflected people's past experiences including an emphasis on the importance of independence and concerns about a new service development.

Family carers (n = 2)

Two family carers were interviewed. One answered questions in respect of her son and the other about her situation as a carer.

The first family carer's son is a young man who has been going through transition, moving on from school to college to day support service. He receives one-to-one outreach support from home and has three days in the day centre. She feels that this arrangement works well. His confidence is slowly being built up.

> "He has really settled here. It has been positive and made a real difference. He knows the routine and the staff know him well and know his needs".

Information about choices for the carer seemed more limited. She had not heard of Direct Payments or advocacy and did not know a short breaks co-ordinator or of any alternative to the respite her son uses six weeks a year.

The son does not attend his review meetings. His mother goes to six monthly meetings and feels that the staff respond positively and that it is easy to make a phone all to discuss anything. She is always consulted before changes are made.

The carer was able to give an example of being able to change something about her son's service.

> "When my son first started travelling by centre bus it was causing anxiety. It was sometimes late or noisy. The arrangements changed to being collected from home by … (name of worker) 2 days and 3 days I get him off the bus at the stop where … (worker) meets us and then I go on to my work. His behaviour has changed now this service is provided."

She reported a "very positive" relationship between her family and the social worker, although she is concerned that they may get a different social worker now her son is receiving adult services. They were given information about what happens after school.

Her son is not independent while out and about and relies on staff or help from home. He has behaviour and communication differences but will speak if he knows someone well. His mother has heard of the Care Commission but not the Mental Welfare Commission.

The son has no current health problems but did experience a serious health problem while at the day centre. The surgery did not respond with urgency and so she arranged to get him to hospital. He was not anxious there, even though there was no contact with the learning disability nurse. Mother and carers have now been trained to use an epipen and advised to call 999 in an emergency for a paramedic to administer medication.

It is a bit early to tell how things will work out for her son. "There have been so many changes we are taking a day at a time".

The second carer cares for her adult son with severe learning disabilities at home. She does not have an advocate but would like one. Her main concern is her social worker whom she feels does not listen. When she required a major operation it took three months to arrange home care. She says that she complained to the social work department and asked for a new social worker but without success. She is also concerned that she has been unable to get her son's name on the tenancy of her house because he cannot sign his name.

Young people (n = 4)

Four young people considered to have severe or complex needs who attended a learning support unit spent an afternoon at the end of term completing part of an exercise to find out about their lives. The exercise (devised for NHS Quality Improvement Scotland reviews) is called "I do stuff". The parts that all the young people had time to complete were:

- This is me (a photograph of themselves);
- Some things I do that make me feel good (pictures cut out of magazines and photographs taken locally were used to illustrate this);
- Some people I know; and
- This is place where I belong.

We are grateful to staff at the learning support unit for making this happen at such short notice. Names have been withheld for confidentiality.

Table 24   Young people's lives

	Things I do that make me feel good	Some people I know	A place where I belong	This is what helps me join in	I want to do more of
First young person	Pictures of dolphin, sports centre	11 names including 6 teachers	I go running with … (name) and tennis. Picture of sports centre, tennis racquet, athletics and bowling.		
Second young person	Pictures of New Zealand, sports centre, football pitch, rugby ball, swimmer and boxing match.	25 names including mum and dad and 10 teachers	Name of town where lives		

Third young person	Three names, my friends, mum, dad. Pictures of dog, clothes, bubble gum, swimming, sports centre and a bowl of pasta.	30 names including 10 teachers, nana, dad, mum and (perhaps) three siblings.		Name of the occupational therapist.	Swimming, MacDonald's, Horse riding.
Fourth young person	Pictures of soaps on TV	… (name of girl) at school and magazine picture of blonde girl.	Name of town where lives.		

The young people identified interests that were typical for their age and especially sports. Their distinct identities and personalities come though even in this short exercise. It did seem as though many of the names they identified were names of others from their school which may indicate more limited social networks than others of their age. They seemed to have a strong sense of belonging to home, family, school and the place that they live.

The booklets they completed will be returned to them through their school.

Conclusions

This is a small sample which limits the generalisations that can be made. However within these limitations a range of services was sampled. The interview findings do show how valuable it is to ask people with learning disabilities themselves what they think.

- **Support and choice**

Good relationships with staff were reported but more choices could be made available.

- **Having a say**

Some people have gained a great deal from participation. The benefits of this should be extended. People could benefit from personal life plans of which they had copies. The profile of advocacy could be increased.

- **Social workers**

Most people reported good relationships and believed their social workers would protect them. Three people said they did not have a social worker.

- **Feeling safe**

All 14 adults said they knew someone they could contact if they were frightened. Very few have heard of the Mental Welfare Commission.

The confidence to go out and about varies. Other people are an important safeguard.

- **Health**

People are aware of healthy lifestyles. There are generally good reports of doctors and hospitals.

- **Quality of life**

Most people reported that they were leading the life they wanted but some had restricted opportunities and networks.

Appendix 1: Co-ordinated care service inspections by the Care Commission

The Care Commission took part in the Borders Follow up Inspection. We co-ordinated inspections of registered care services used by people with learning disabilities in the Borders.

Coordinated care service inspections

We looked at 56 services within the Borders area, which are largely or solely used by people with learning disabilities. We risk assessed services based on issues raised in the Social Work Services Inspectorate and Mental Welfare Commission reports.

We identified eleven services to inspect at the same time as the follow up inspection. We visited them over a 3 week period beginning the week before and ending the week after the joint inspection. We made 6 unannounced inspections and 5 announced inspections.

We used pre-inspection material and self evaluations by services against regulations. Services also commented on relevant National Care Standards. We used questions provided by the Scottish Consortium for Learning Disability to seek the views of people with learning disabilities. We interviewed staff during inspection visits. We gave out a questionnaire to look at how well Scottish Borders Council raised awareness of the Social Services Council Codes of Practice.

We inspected these services during the period 2 May 2005 and 22 May 2005.

CS Number	Service Name	Location	Type of service	Type of inspection	Case Number	Report Available on CC website
CS2003009177	Garvald – West Linton	West Linton	Care Home Service	Unannounced	2005102465	No
CS2003009154	Aberlour – 4 St Cuthbert Drive	St Boswells	Care Home Service	Unannounced	2005094568	No
CS2003009156	Ark – Kelso Project	Kelso	Care Home Service	Unannounced	2005096960	No
CS2003043939	Lennel House care home	Coldstream	Care Home Service	Unannounced	2005093456	No
CS2003009200	Streets ahead - West Core	Hawick	Care Home Service	Announced	2005093460	Yes
CS2003010303	St Aidans – care home	Gattonside	Care Home Service	Unannounced	2005094580	No
CS2003017906	Lanark Lodge – day care	Duns	Support Service	Announced	2005093445	No
CS2003009186	Gala day service	Galashiels	Support Service	Announced	2005093481	Yes
CS2003017967	Victoria park day Centre	Peebles	Support Service	Announced	2005094092	No
CS2003009160	BOC - Connections	Selkirk	Support Service	Unannounced	2005096967	No
CS2004056959	Streets ahead – (Borders) – Hawick - care at home/Housing Support	Hawick	Combined Care at Home and Housing Support Service	Announced	2005094688	Yes

Inspection results

We found all the inspected care services are making progress in dealing with recommendations and requirements from previous reports. We found all care services have lots of strengths. In all care services people with learning disabilities said they were happy with the service. We found carers were involved in services. Most services were fully staffed to meet their conditions of registration. All services knew about National Care Standards and were trying to meet them.

We found the majority of care services and all of the inspected care home services have areas for further development. Our reports say some people with learning disabilities don't have written agreements about what to expect from services. Some people with learning disabilities were not involved in how the service was delivered. We found a need for effective risk assessment and management, especially on fire safety matters. We found only one care service where staff didn't know about the Social Services Code of Practice. We commented on staff selection, support and training in the majority of care services.

We made 10 requirements - *A requirement is a statement setting out an enforceable action required of a service provider in order that the service comply with current legislation, usually within a specific timescale.*

We made 50 recommendations - *A recommendation is a statement setting out proposed actions to be taken by the service provider aimed at improving the quality of service (based on good practice and professional judgement) but which would not be subject to enforcement action if not actioned.*

Only one care service, *Streets Ahead – West Core,* had no recommendations or requirements. All other services have provided action plans with timescales to address the matters raised. We will monitor implementation of these action plans by:

- follow on regulatory visits; and

- inspections later in the year for care home services.

A copy of the full report of each inspection is available on the Care Commission website www.carecommission.com. It is available from Compass House 11 Riverside Drive, Dundee DD1 4AN or from the local office at Galabank Mill, Wilderhaugh Trading Estate, Galashiels TD1 1PR.

Conclusion

We found care services for people with learning disabilities in the Borders are making progress. We will continue to monitor this. We will see if services meet the needs of people with learning disabilities and their families. We will find out if services are socially inclusive.

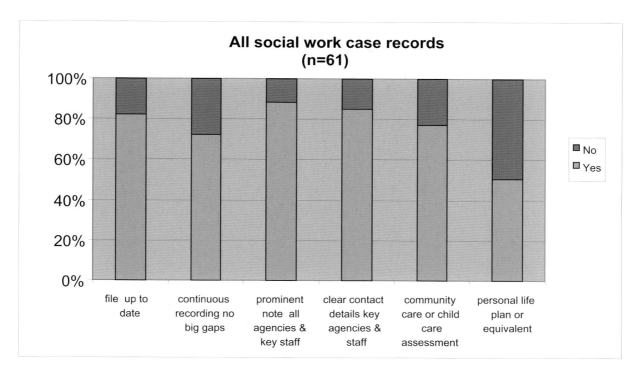

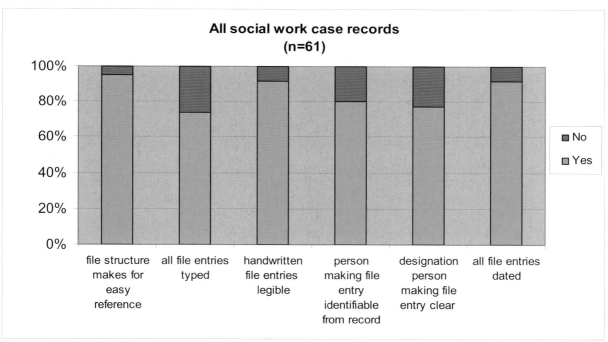

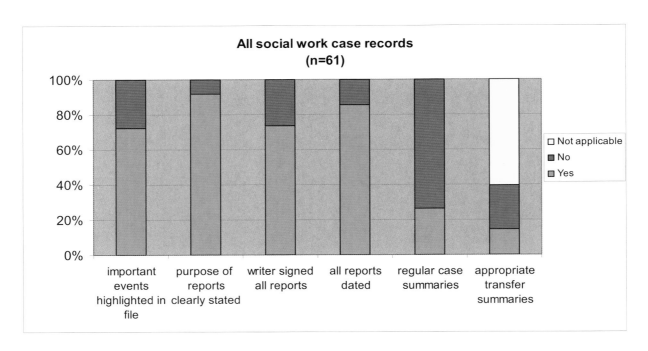

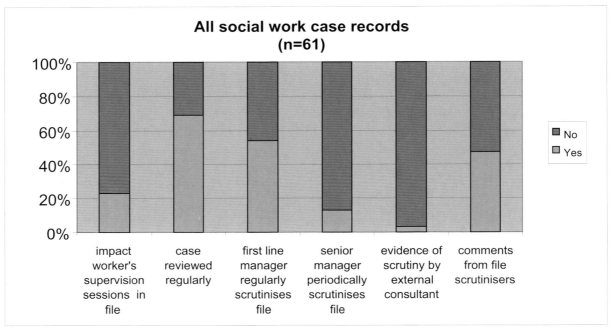

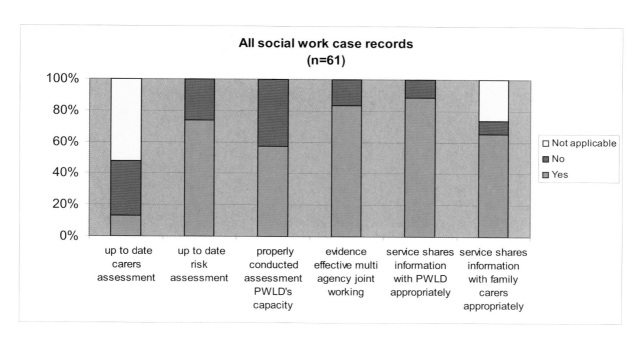

All social work case records
(n=61)

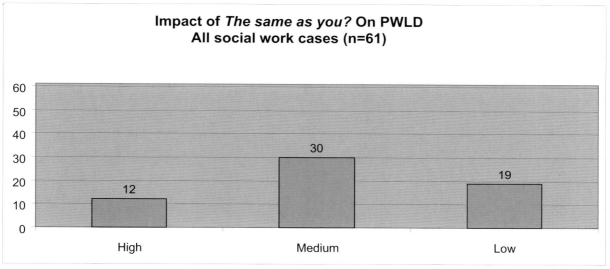

Impact of *The same as you?* On PWLD
All social work cases (n=61)

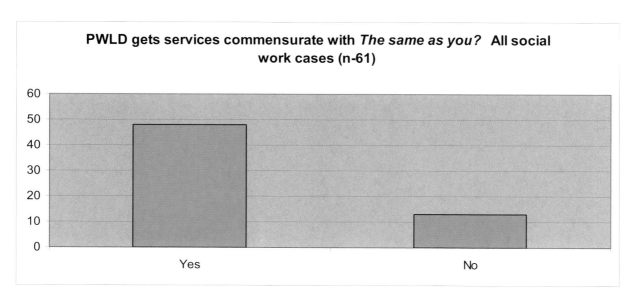

PWLD gets services commensurate with *The same as you?* All social
work cases (n-61)

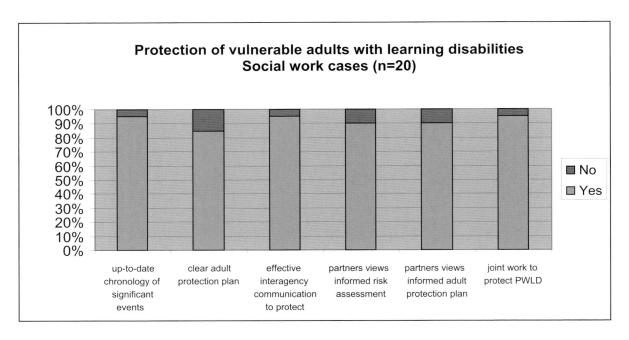

Protection of vulnerable adults with learning disabilities
Social work cases (n=20)

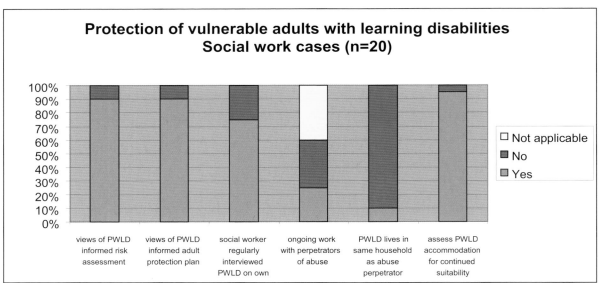

Protection of vulnerable adults with learning disabilities
Social work cases (n=20)

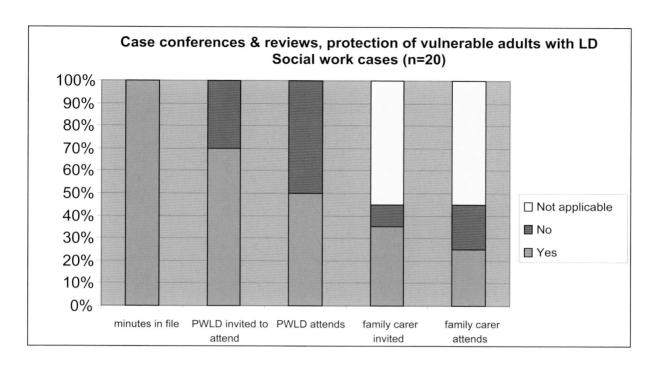

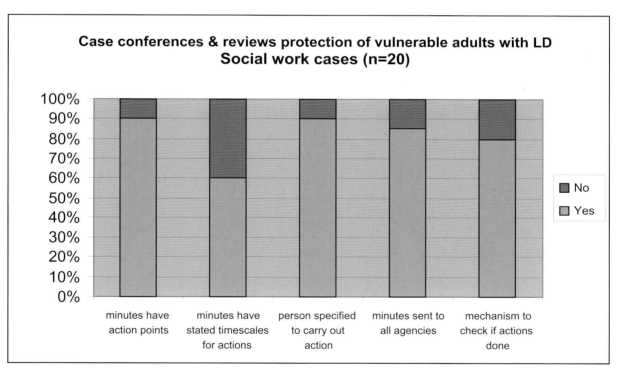

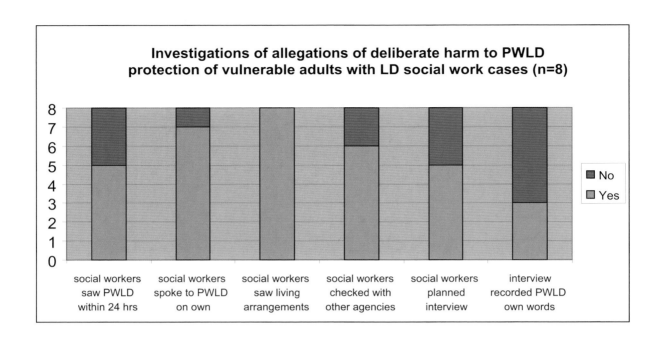

Investigations of allegations of deliberate harm to PWLD protection of vulnerable adults with LD social work cases (n=8)

Legend: ■ No   ■ Yes

Categories:
- social workers saw PWLD within 24 hrs
- social workers spoke to PWLD on own
- social workers saw living arrangements
- social workers checked with other agencies
- social workers planned interview
- interview recorded PWLD own words

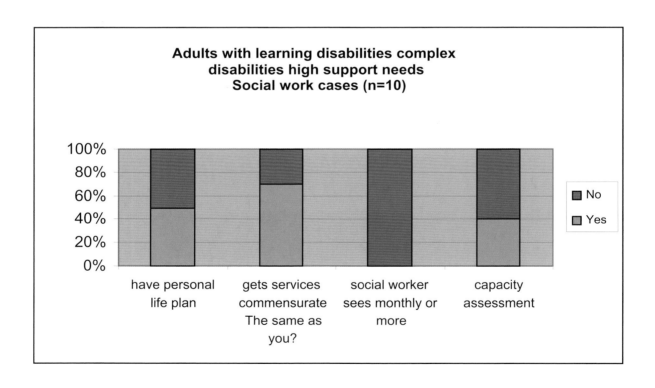

Adults with learning disabilities complex disabilities high support needs Social work cases (n=10)

Legend: ■ No   ■ Yes

Categories:
- have personal life plan
- gets services commensurate The same as you?
- social worker sees monthly or more
- capacity assessment

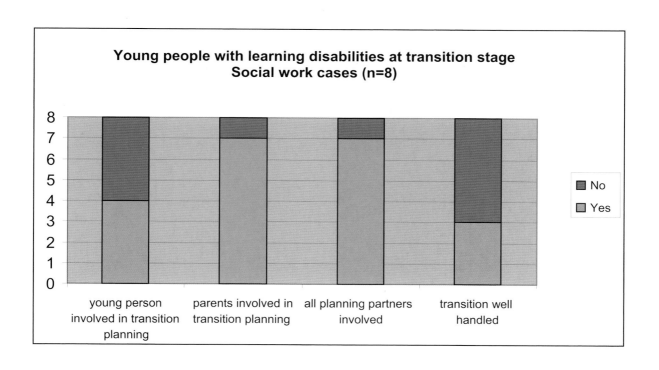

Appendix 3: List of documents submitted by Scottish Borders Council

Management of protection of vulnerable adults

Partnership documents

NHS Borders/ Scottish Borders Council update on progress and evidence table 7April 2005.

NHS Borders/ Scottish Borders Council update on progress and evidence table recommendations 1 to 12.

Definition of vulnerable adult.

Inter-agency Steering Group Minutes:
- 5 November 2004,
- 14 January 2005,
- 18 February 2005.

Scottish Borders Council

Scottish Borders Council Vulnerable Adult Procedures.

Council Report on establishment of Vulnerable Adults Protection and Reviewing Unit – 29 June 2004.

Remit/constitution of the Vulnerable Adults Committee:-
- Report to Executive (4 May 2004),
- Report to Executive (17 February 2004),
- Vulnerable Adult Group Structure diagram.

Documentation on the audit of staff knowledge of the Vulnerable Adults Policy:-
- Report March 2005,
- Summary of key issues,
- Evaluation of the revised training programmes 2003 & 2004.

Selection of initial and review vulnerable adults case conference minutes.

Adult Protection Committee proposals and details of the governance arrangements.

Minutes of the Adult Protection Committee and relevant reports to the APC.

NHS Borders

Primary and community services toolkit for vulnerable adults (24 April 2005).

Progress against Mental Welfare Commission action plan– update for Director of Nursing and Midwifery.

Transfer of care for vulnerable adults – flowchart.

Policy, Procedure and guidance

Partnership documents

Partnership in Practice 2004–2007.

Revised Critical Information Exchange Protocol.

Joint Dispute Resolution Procedure.

Report on implementation of Dispute Resolution Protocol.

Role and Function of the Borders Learning Disability Service (including Learning Disability Core Management Team Roles and Responsibilities).

Care Programme Approach – Joint LD Team Operational Guidelines.

Draft Plan of Joint Learning Disability Service.

Facilitating Police Interviewing of those with a Mental Disorder – The Role of the Appropriate Adult.

Integrating Care Management & the Care Programme Approach – A Proposal for Harmonising Arrangements.

Learning Disability Strategy Group Proposal for Joint Health and Social Work Commissioning Group.

Scottish Borders Council & NHS Borders Framework for Meeting the Health & Social Care Needs of People with Learning Disabilities.

NHS Borders & Scottish Borders Council Information Sharing Protocol Consent Form – Sharing of Information.

Operational Organisational Development and Training Plan for Joint Learning Disability Service.

Project Planning Arrangements Learning Disability Service Integration.

Proposal for an aligned budget for learning disability services. Brief for Learning Disability Strategy Group 26 November 2004.

Scottish Borders Council & NHS Borders Learning Disabilities Integration Project – Project Log.

Scottish Borders Council & NHS Borders Learning Disabilities Integration Project – Project Manager's Report 01/12/04.

Scottish Borders Council and NHS Borders Outline Commissioning Plan for Adults with Learning Disabilities 29 October 2004.

Framework for meeting the Health and Social Care Needs of People with Learning Disabilities.

Scottish Borders Council

Case Recording Guidelines.

Risk Assessment Framework.

Procedures for the Emergency Duty Team.

Case Transfer Procedure.

Case Transfer Summary.

Details of the monitoring of the Case Transfer Procedure.

Carers assessment - Short guide to help complete carers assessment form.

Policy and Procedures for implementation of the Adults with Incapacity Act 2000.

NHS Borders

Guidelines: Protecting Vulnerable Adults.

Learning Disability Service Health Assessment.

Learning Disability Services Initial Nursing Assessment & Hume Unit: Admission Criteria, Care Philosophy, etc.

Child Health Strategy December 2004 (Draft 1 for Discussion).

Community Nursing Records – Documentation Standards and Good Practice Guidelines.

Draft Proposal for Joint Treatment and Assessment Service.

Draft Report on Children with Learning Disabilities who have Complex Needs July 2004.

Health Improvement Strategy for People with Learning Disabilities (Draft 2 25.3.05).

Inpatient Redesign Group Hume Re-provision Proposals Paper to Mental Health and Learning Disabilities Clinical Board Draft Version 2.

Investment in Learning Disability Services 2004/05.

Learning disability Complex Care Packages Draft Process.

Learning Disabilities Services and Resources 2004-2005.

Learning Disabilities Strategy Development Day 17 June 2004.

Learning Disability Assertive Outreach Assessment and Treatment Service.

Local Health Care Co-operative Action Plan (from Mental Welfare Commission Investigation).

Patient Discharge Policy and Procedures (Borders General Hospital) January 2005.

Completion of health records policy, April 2005.

Roles and Clinical Responsibilities of the Specialist Learning Disability Service.

Finance

Partnership documents

Scottish Borders Council/ NHS Borders: Scoping of AWLD Joint Resourcing Pot 2004-2005.

Copies of overheads on Investment in learning disability service 2003-2004; 2005-2006 (compared to inflation) and list of new posts.

Report to Well-Being Partnership Board (20 April 2005): Joint Future Aligned Budget Report.

NHS Borders and Scottish Borders Council: Financial Protocol to cover Joint Working and Aligned Budgets.

Scottish Borders Council

Budget Preparation for financial year 2004-2005 - Improvement Fund.

Social Work Revenue Budget 2005-2006   (incorporating "Same as You" funds).

Social Work: 2004-2005 Health Board Resource Transfer.

Social Work Annual Report of Services Purchased by Scottish Borders Council using Resources Transferred from NHS Borders. (April 2003 to March 2004).

Quality assurance

Partnership

Details of the further case review of cases where there is joint working with NHS Borders: multi-agency audit of case notes for complex individuals with a learning disability (January 2005).

Monitoring and audit of Adults with Incapacity Act implementation.

Scottish Borders Council

Quality Assurance Strategy.

Practice Standards document (Nov. 2004).

Review of Vulnerable Adults Procedures.

Framework for Case File Auditing.

Procedure for the systematic review of all learning disability case files. Details of the audit template.

Social Work Learning Disability File Audit – summary of findings, action plan and report to elected members (June 2004).

Sample of reports about the random sampling of case files that go to the Chief Social Work Officer and the Director of Social Work Services.

Details of the audit of case files carried out by the independent advisor:
- Vulnerable Adult Social Work Practice Case Audit – Aim & Task,
- Audit Report 1,
- Audit Report 2,
- Audit Report 3,
- Letter of agreement with Independent Adviser.

Details of the regular review of case files:
- Recording Audit Report – Adult Day Services,
- Response to Recording Audit Report (Adult Day Services),
- Recording Audit Report – Day Services for Older People,
- Recording Audit Report – Residential Homes for Older People.

Details of compliance monitoring by accountable line managers and the Vulnerable Adults Unit.

Sample of Supervision Notes from Group Manager (Community Care).

Records of Critical Incident Reviews.

NHS Borders

Accountability Review – August 2004.

Audit of Staff with a Personal Development Plan.

Confidential TNA Report Organisation Learning & Development Needs September 2003.

Healthcare Governance Report (February 2005).

Self-assessment for NHS QIS Quality Indicator 3 March 2005.

NHS QIS Review of Learning Disability Services in NHS Borders, February 2005.

Notes of Interagency Adult Protection Subgroup 30/07/04 .

Human resources, training and staff development

Partnership

Draft Operational Organisational Development and Training Plan for Joint Learning Disability Service.

Notes of Meeting of Learning Disability Training Forum 11 November 2004.

Scottish Consortium for Learning Disability and Scottish Borders Council: Setting the Context – Making Good Things Happen Training Pack.

Training Programme – Preparation for the New Integrated Learning Disability Service.

Investigation to case conference: training programme.

Job Description Joint Learning Disability Services Manager Post.

Details of joint interview training with health and the police.

Appropriate Adult Training programme.

Details of Mental Health Officer Training programme and evaluation.

Details of training programme (devised by the Interagency Group) for implementation of the Mental Health (Care & Treatment) (Scotland) Act 2003.

Scottish Borders Council

Action Plan and report to Council regarding implementation on the Scottish Social Services Council Codes of Practice, February 2004.

Workforce Planning & Development: Action Plan for 2005/2006.

Training Plan for 2004/05.

Review of Training Plan – August 2004.

Single shared assessment training programme.

Social Work Memorandum re Proposed Training Policy and Programme of Development for all Staff working in Adult Services for People with Learning Disabilities.

Supervision Policy and Supervision Policy Standards, November 2004.

Specimen Job Descriptions:
- Day Services Review Officer,
- Social Care Assistant,
- Rapid Response Professional.

Induction Arrangements:
- Community Care Induction Pack,
- Corporate Induction Pack,
- Induction Proposal Paper – first draft.

NHS Borders

Audit of staff with a personal development plan.

Draft statutory and mandatory training requirements – mental health and learning disability network.

Confidential Training Needs Analysis Report Mental Health & Learning Disabilities Oct 2003.

Dietician for learning disability service: additional information.

Training and Professional Development Plan/ Directory 2005-2007.

Training & Professional Development Learning Plan/ Directory 2004.

Training & Professional Development Learning Plan/ Directory 2005-2007.

Protecting Vulnerable Adults Awareness Sessions Schedule.

Internal audit – appraisal & personal development planning – March/ April 2005.

Job descriptions and person specifications:
- Primary Care/Acute Learning Disability Liaison Nurse,
- Community Dietician for Learning Disability,
- Mental Health Act Facilitator Post,
- Primary Care/Acute Learning Disability Liaison Nurse,
- Clinical Services Manager,

Other documents

Partnership

"I'll Show You" Scottish Borders Symbols Dictionary Project.

Borders Child Protection Committee Interagency Child Protection Guidelines.

Report to Scottish Borders Well-being Partnership Board (20 April 2005).

Directory of services for children with additional needs in the Scottish Borders.

Bright New Futures Strategy Summary.

Bright New Futures News letter February 2005.

Report by the Scottish Borders Council and NHS Borders entitled 'Report on Multi-agency procedures for Transition from children to Adult services for young people with a disability,' April 2005.

Notes of Promoting Health Supporting Inclusion Steering Group 31/03/04, 14/05/04, 28/05/04, 11/06/04, 25/06/04, 09/07/04.

Scottish Borders Autism Team - Annual Report 2003-2004.

Scottish Borders Health and Care Partnership Service User and Carer Involvement Strategy.

Mental health and learning disability network update on role and function of borders learning disability service.

Role, Remit and membership of Transitions Working Group.

Scottish Borders Council

Report entitled 'Integrated Children and Young People's Services Plan' produced by Scottish Borders Council By the Director of Education and Lifelong Learning 21 April 2005.

Community Care Restructuring document.

Social Work Management Information System Delivery timetable.

Service level agreement between social work and legal services.

Eligibility Criteria for Community Care Services.

Whistle-blowing Policy.

Her Majesty's Inspector of Education (HMIe) Inspection report on the educational functions of Scottish Borders Council, August 2002.

Letter to Scottish Borders Council Chief Executive from HMIe – Interim follow up inspection of the educational functions of Scottish Borders Council December 2003.

HMIe Follow Up Inspection of the educational functions of the Local authority: report January 2005.

'Access All Areas:' report produced by Berwickshire High School in November 2003 Summary of Good Practice in Scottish Borders Schools re primary – secondary transition and secondary – post – sixteen transitions.

Additional support for learning document, April 2003.

Service Integration for Adults with Learning Disabilities Strategic Plan Draft 2, 29 October 2004.

Social Work Department Annual Report April 2003 – March 2004.

NHS Borders

Development of Community Children's Nursing Team.

Clinical Governance Annual Report April 2003 – March 2004.

Clinical Governance Organisational Chart.

Health Improvement for People with Learning Disabilities: Paper to Joint Commissioning Team (Learning Disabilities).

Music therapy service: Children's services.

NHS Borders Development of Community Children's Nursing Team.

NHS Borders Services for Adults and Children with a Learning Disability in the Scottish Borders: A Healthcare Needs Assessment.

NHS Health Scotland Learning Disability Health Needs Assessment Report (NHS 2004).

Performance Assessment Framework Patient Focus Public Involvement Implementation Plan 2004 – 2007.

Primary Care/ Acute Learning Disability Liaison Nurse Documentation: 12 Month work plan, flowcharts.

Care of Patient with a Learning Disability attending the Acute Hospital (i) Elective Admission and (ii) Out-Patient Attendance (from NHS Lothian to be adapted for NHS Borders).

Promoting Health Supporting Inclusion Conference 27 April 2004. Documentation and Presentations.

Records of Dietetic Input to Learning Disability Services.

Report on Draft Child Health Strategy.

Roles & Responsibilities of Primary Care Staff where there is Multidisciplinary Involvement.

Vacancy management & recruitment – policy statement.

Patient discharge policy, January 2005.

Primary care/acute learning disability liaison nurse – 12 month work plan.

Guidelines for records and record keeping – nursing midwifery council.

Appendix 4: Borders Follow Up Inspection Team

Ian Kerr, lead inspector, Social Work Inspection Agency.
Marc Hendrikson, inspector, Social Work Inspection Agency.
Stuart Bond, inspector, Social Work Inspection Agency.
Prof. Juliet Cheetham, sessional inspector, Social Work Inspection Agency.
Ken Logan, administrator, Social Work Inspection Agency.
Susan Fallon, inspection project manager, Social Work Inspection Agency.
Margaret Anne Gilbert, social work officer, Mental Welfare Commission.
Nell Laing, locality manager, Care Commission.
Dr Martin Campbell, NHS, Quality Improvement Scotland, senior teaching fellow, University of St Andrews.
Brian Rosie, inspector, People First Scotland.
Mary Anderson, inspector, People First Scotland.
Ursula Corker, inspector, Carers Scotland.
Anna Boni, inspector, HM Inspectorate of Education.
Anne Stoker, inspector, HM Inspectorate of Education.

The following team members were present for part of the inspection visit (May 9-13).

Dr Donald Lyons, director of the Mental Welfare Commission.
Gill Ottley, depute chief inspector, Social Work Inspection Agency.
Pat Mulrooney, staff officer, HM Inspectorate of Constabulary.
John Davidson, locality manager, Care Commission.
Tony Jevon, social work officer, Mental Welfare Commission.
Dr Flora Sinclair, medical officer, Mental Welfare Commission.
Selina Clinch, senior project officer, NHS, Quality Improvement Scotland,
Audit Scotland.

People First Scotland Support Workers.

Kate Milliken.
Fiona Wilkinson.
Margaret Shovlin, personal carer.